INTRODUCTION TO THE GREAT RELIGIONS

Jean Daniélou, S.J. et al.

Close contact between the major religions of the world has become a fact of life. Both individual relationships and religious writings have made this confrontation between religions a daily occurrence.

Political realities, too, have given the encounter between religions a special importance. Buddhism in Southeast Asia, Hinduism in India, Islam in the Middle East, atheism in the Communist nations and the nature religions in Africa all have become increasingly influential factors in the relations between nations. This has given impetus to the study of these religions as a prerequisite for maintaining world peace.

But the most far-reaching purpose for becoming acquainted with the great non-Christian religions of the world is to further the cause of ecumenism. Such
study will not only
commun
can serv
Christia
apprecia
of the de

The book ... timely and intriguing picture of the varied religious beliefs which men accept and live by and is a source for a more mature perspective on the Christian religion.

INTRODUCTION TO THE GREAT RELIGIONS

INTRODUCTION TO THE GREAT RELIGIONS

Jean Danielou, S.J.
Andre Retif, S.J.
Joseph Hours, S.J.
Francois Houang
Maurice Queguiner, P.F.M.
R. P. Dunoyer, P.F.M.
R. P. Demann
Gaston Fessard, S.J.

Translated by Albert J. La Mothe, Jr.

FIDES PUBLISHERS, INC.
NOTRE DAME, INDIANA

Nihil Obstat: Louis J. Putz, C.S.C.
University of Notre Dame

Imprimatur: Leo A. Pursley, D.D.
Bishop of Fort Wayne-South Bend

Published originally in France by
CERCLE ST. JEAN-BAPTISTE,
12 Rue St. J.B. De LaSalle, Paris.

Library of Congress Catalog Card Number: 64-16499

CONTENTS

1. Danielou	Christianity and the Non-Christian Religions	7
2. Retif	The Religions of Nature	29
3. Hours	Islam	41
4. Houang	Buddhism	57
5. Queguiner	Hinduism	67
6. Dunoyer	The Religions of Japan	85
7. Demann	Judaism	111
8. Fessard	Contemporary Atheism	121
9. Danielou	The Transcendence of Christianity	133

1. JEAN DANIELOU, S.J.

CHRISTIANITY AND THE NON-CHRISTIAN RELIGIONS

In this introduction to a comparative study of religions, I will attempt to give an overall perspective which will do justice to the values of the various religions and, at the same time, respect the differences of nature and order among them.

Today we are witnessing an inevitable confrontation of religions. On the personal level we are continually encountering representatives of other religions and on the literary level religious writings from the Baghavat Gita to the Koran or the mystics of Israel are readily available. This phenomenon is a characteristic part of the life of contemporary man.

This contact can give rise to two dangerous attitudes. The first is a sectarianism that makes us look with disdain upon religions different from our own and render severe and simplistic judgments on them. This attitude used to be common, but occurs less frequently these days. Yet how many people still have crude ideas about the religions of Africa, for instance? In the past, it took the excellent works of a man like Father Aupiais, a great initiator of research on the African religions, to bring the missionary world to appreciate the religious worth of these religions, where they often were pictured as nothing but a collection of superstitions and more or less barbaric rites. It is, then, necessary to know and understand the values of all religions simply to meet standards of intelligence and culture. This would serve to counteract what would otherwise be a closed, unintelligent attitude of hostility.

There is another opposite danger which is more serious and more frequent today: this is the danger of syncretism.

There are, I believe, few religious poems more beautiful than the Baghavat Gita, the Hindu chant of the blessed. It cannot but arouse the love of God and detachment from the things of the world. The Enneads of Plotinus, to name a Greek mystic, are unquestionably a work of very high religious value. The poems of El Helladj, translated by Massignon, are also among the most beautiful of mystical poems and bear comparison with the hymn of St. John of the Cross. In addition, we find members of non-Christian religions whose sincerity and authenticity are striking; they are high religious personalities, worthy of our admiration and our respect, from whom we can draw excellent lessons in the matter of the spirit of prayer or of charity for one's neighbor.

All this is quite true, but it may lead many of our contemporaries to see in the various religions just so many different paths for reaching God. Perhaps differences of degree will be acknowledged among the religions, but they will all be considered equally valid. And it will be added that a truly free, tolerant and open attitude demands that this diversity be allowed.

This more or less syncretist attitude is false, not only from the point of view of the true scale of religious values, but even from the scientific point of view. An authentic objective examination of religions brings us to a realization of the fundamental differences, differences in structure, among the various types of religions.

We shall therefore attempt a comparison centering around three great problems:

a) *The concept which the religions have of God,* which goes to the very substance of religion.
b) The notion they have developed about the *way of access to God*:
In what does the fundamental religious experience consist?
In what does the religion consist from man's point of view?
c) From the point of view of time, what is their *concept of history*? This is important in the differences of structure among the various religions.

I. *Concept of God of the different religions*

We must distinguish at the outset among three main groups:

The cosmic religions. I prefer this word to two other expressions which are sometimes used: "pagan religions," because the word "pagan" implies a certain pejorative character; and "natural religions," because the term "natural" is rather equivocal, to the extent that it is connected with a certain philosophy which opposes nature to grace, something which is outside our scope. On the other hand, the term "cosmic" essentially expresses a knowledge of God through His manifestation in the cosmos, in the world, in nature.

Among these religions, we will find both superior religions (such as Hinduism) and religions of a more elementary structure (such as certain African or Oceanian religions).

The Biblical religions: Judaism and Islam, whose common points and points of difference we shall have to specify later.

The Christian religions, that is, the different denominations connected with Christ: Orthodoxy, Catholicism, and the multiple forms of Protestantism, which, in today's world, represent a considerable array.

1) *The concept of God in the cosmic religions*

It is in this area that the history of religions has made the most remarkable progress particularly during the past fifty years. The work of historians of religion in the 19th century initially consisted in amassing an immense amount of material. One of the characteristic products of this era is the famous book by Sir James Frazer, *The Golden Bough,* which, in a series of enormous volumes, devotes itself to all the forms of rites, all the forms of sacrifices, all the forms of myths, in a kind of disarray admittedly disconcerting at first glance.

Nevertheless, this work has rendered a great service. Someone had to make a start with a descriptive account so that people would know what they were talking about. There are also some admirable works dealing with both the past and the present. For certain African tribes, we can cite the recent books by Pastor Leenhardt and Griaule. From these we have documentation of incomparable value.

In a second phase, there was an attempt to interpret this accumulated material in terms of certain preconceived ideas. This was the time—really rather ominous—when a whole collection of so-called explanatory theories arose, such as the sociological theory of Durkheim and his school, which interpreted religion as the result of social pressure on individuals.

It should be emphasized that there is nothing in common between the sociology of religions and the sociological interpretation of religion. The sociology of religions is a completely valid scientific technique, whereas the sociological interpretation of religions, which reduces religion to a sociological datum, is a thoroughly questionable thesis. It is to this same category that we must assign the Marxist interpretations which make religion the projection of the economic contradictions of society into a world of fantasy. Eliminating these sociological contradictions would therefore result in the elimination of religion. This is a highly simplistic concept which no serious historian accepts today.

More interesting to us may be those theories—such as those of Jung and the school of depth psychology—which see in religion the expression of an unconscious underlying man's psychology which, projecting itself into myths, turns out to be the expression of the obscure depth of the human soul.

These forms of interpretation have been left behind by the works of more modern historians of religion. Three great names must be pointed out: Rudolph Otto, in his famous book, *The Sacred*; Van der Leeuw, in his *Phenomenology of Religions*; and finally, Mircea Eliade, an Orthodox Rumanian who published in French a whole series of extremely interesting books (he is also a novelist) put out by Payot and by Gallimard, in particular, *History of Religions* (Payot).

The characteristic method of this school has been to bring out the irreducible character of the sacred, of that which corresponds in man to the experience of the divine, which cannot be reduced to sociological pressure, nor to psychological sublimation, but which contains an absolutely original idea. Otto has described this marvelously under the expressions in the different religions, from the most elementary to the most elevated, the symbols they employ, the heading of the *tremendum*, that is, that which inspires terror (the most basic form of the sacred), the Latin *pavor*. It has to do with the total disorder which seizes man in the face of something absolutely unusual which thoroughly disorients him. This reality is what the Hindus call the "completely different." This fear is not the fear of some danger, but the trembling which seizes us when God comes too close to us.

At a more advanced stage, God appears as the majesty and the infinite grandeur which throw man into a sentiment of veneration, of respect, of reverence, of adoration.

Finally, there comes the discovery of God as holiness, which represents the supreme deepening of this fundamental experience. God appears then as infinite value, arousing love and at the same time, making man become aware of his status as sinner, of his state of impurity. At this point, we think of Isaias: "Holy, Holy, Holy, Lord God of Hosts," and: "Woe is me, for my lips are defiled"—an admirable testimony of the experience of the sacred in its highest form, of the awareness which man acquires of his own misery, of his basic impurity when the holiness of God approaches him.

Compared to this vision, all the sociological, psychological or psychoanalytical explanations no longer exist, so near are we to a privileged area of human experience, that which we find in the great religious geniuses of mankind and which constitutes an order entirely unto itself, the mysterious universe of the experience of God.

We must point out that we are still at a strictly descriptive, phenomenological, scientific, level, which as yet implies no theological aspect whatsoever.

A new phase was begun by Van der Leeuw and Eliade when they demonstrated that if one compares the religious images they utilize, the myths by which they express themselves, one discovers some extraordinary analogies. The enormous and inorganic inventory of the first historians of religion is becoming organized. Without any influence of one upon the other, the same forms of expression are everywhere found at the level of the cosmic religions. This leads to a very remarkable conclusion, namely that there is an objective value in the symbols; that they do not seem to be conventional inventions of the human spirit; that the same realities of the cosmos manifest for men in all religions the same aspects of God.

This is what Mircea Eliade has called the "hierophanies" (*hieros*=sacred). For the man of the cosmic religions, the entire cosmos is, in Claudel's expression, "a book that speaks to us of God."

Eliade explains that nothing would be more inaccurate than to imagine that the pagans adore rocks, pieces of wood, the sun as a star, the moon as a planet, etc. If an inhabitant of Mars arriving on earth one day enters a Catholic church, would not his first impression be that people are adoring statues of stone, a piece of bread, a cup of wine? Seen from the outside, would not Catholicism seem as rude an idolatry as that which we attribute to the African religions? We have to render the same justice we would claim for ourselves to the non-Christian religions, including the most elementary. There is in reality among the men of all religions a far more mysterious idea of God than we imagine. The visible signs are to be considered not as ends of adoration, but as manifestations of the mystery, as hierophanies.

Here are some examples of hierophanies:

—The starry sky, in all religions, appears as the expression of the permanence of God in the regularity of its movement, as opposed to the atmosphere which surrounds the earth, which is characterized by its perpetual changeableness. Have we not retained the expression "heaven" to designate the divine places? We have borrowed it from this hierophanic symbolism. When we say that after death we shall go to heaven, it does not mean, except for the Pythagoreans, that we are going to the stars.

—The thunderstorm is an exceptional theophany: the storm makes the terror pass away. In certain French country areas, when the thunder peals, the women make the sign of the Cross. At that point they are being far more intelligent than the little primary scientist who laughs at them, saying that it is only a matter of the coming together of positive electricity and negative electricity, forgetting the sacramental dimension which is part of the essence of things. In this sense, it may be said that the monstrous aberration of the modern world lies in its having secularized the cosmos, retaining only its purely scientific aspect and failing to recognize its symbolic and sacred aspect. The pagans had a more profound sense of things than many of our contemporary atheists. Thus the Africans have often kept this elementary sense of the sacred which confers on them a certain facility for resisting our lay, profane, totally secularized spirit. In point of fact, there is in the thunderstorm something which expresses the irresistible power of God. This appears also in the Bible. The thunderstorm there is eminently hierophanic. Yahweh shows Himself on Sinai in thunder and fire, which signify His brilliant and irresistible power.

—The rock. Eliade, in a remarkable passage, shows us the theophanic value of the rock: first of all, because of its permanence. Men pass away, the rock remains. And then, too, because of its resistance: everything breaks on the rock.

And finally, because of its solidity: one can lean on it and it will not give way nor will it yield. "Rock" is one of the names of Yahweh in the Old Testament, and we find it again in the New Testament to express the solidity of Christ Himself.

Eliade has also noted that, in all the religions, not only do the symbols have similar meanings, but they are grouped in an analogous manner. He has, for example, an astonishing section on the theme of the moon, the serpent, and still water. In numerous myths, these three elements are found in association, all three connected with an idea of fecundity, an exaltation of the mystery of life. The serpent is, moreover, eyerywhere a symbol of fertility. This is why it has a disastrous role in Genesis. The account of Genesis is a polemic against the nature cults of Canaan. It is because the serpent has a beneficent role in all the religions of the time that it is given a maleficent role by the Scriptures—it must be shown that it is wrong to adore it, to set it thereby in opposition to the true God. Still, in the brass serpent, a few pages later, the serpent has a beneficent role—Moses had therefore retained the memory of a positive value in the theme of the serpent.

We may note that the poets instinctively rediscover some of these symbols or groups of symbols. This, in fact, derives from a certain perception of the symbolic dimension of things. The gift of the poet very often coincides with the gift of the religious man. But, for the religious man, the symbolism is not something arbitrary or gratuitous, but it is the perception of a mysterious reality which manifests itself under various aspects.

The cosmic religions are essentially the discovery of God through His manifestation in the hierophanies of the universe. This is why they are basically, in their roots, religions of nature. The rhythm of natural life constitutes their fundamental source.

2) *The concept of God in the biblical religions*

A vital moment: we are passing from the world of religions to what can be called the world of revelation. Here we may recall the words of Guardini in *The Lord*: "The worst enemy of revelation is religion." At first glance paradoxical, this statement contains a profound truth: the worst error one can make regarding revelation is to make a religion of it. The worst misunderstanding of Christianity or of Judaism is to make them religions among other religions—the very error of syncretism.

With Judaism and Christianity, we are no longer in the order of religions. We have reached an altogether different level. How are we to define this movement? Generally speaking, that which characterizes religions, is *the seeking of God by man*, through His manifestation in the world. Moreover, it is in this respect that all religions are equally true. For instance, one cannot say that Hinduism is more true than Taoism, that the ancient religions of Africa are truer than the religions of Oceania. At the pagan level, syncretism is correct: here it is a question of parallel, equivalent, endeavors which, consequently, have a perfect right to enrich one another.

On this level, if we were to try to define what the religious heritage of the West is—making a strictly scientific comparison with Hinduism, Taoism, the ancient religions of Africa—we would have to say that we derive from Greco-Latin paganism, related to Hinduism. When Antoine Meillet, my teacher at the Collège de France, used to reconstruct the Indo-European civilization, he insisted strongly on the interconnection between Hinduism, Greece, and the ancient Latin world. The Greek Zeus, the Latin Jupiter, are found in Hinduism; *jnana*, knowledge, is the same word as the Greek *gnosis*, which is the knowledge of God; the Latin *flamen*, priest, is the *brahma*. We have been pagans like the rest.

It is not Christianity which is the religion of the West—it is its old paganism which, after all, is not inferior to the others. The religion of Plato, the religion of Plotinus, the religion of Virgil—all this is comparable to the Baghavat Gita, the great philosophies of Shankara or Matva.

With revelation, we enter a world which is absolutely new. It is no longer a question of man's search for God, *but of God's quest for man*. Revelation is not movement by man in search of God, but *act* of God coming to meet man.

This is why the essential part of revelation has to do with facts, with interventions by God, with acts of God in history. The holy books of the biblical religions, the Old and New Testaments, are essentially histories, whereas the holy books of the pagan religions are basically myths. The essence of the Bible is sacred history, that is, the covenant of God with Abraham, the liberation of the people of Israel by Yahweh, His dwelling in the temple. These are interventions by God in the world of men. It is not necessary at all to be a Christian or a Jew to believe that God exists. The pagans believe that. But it is necessary to be Jew or Christian to believe that God intervened in human existence, that He thereby penetrated into the sphere of the world: this is the history of salvation, through which God manifests Himself in a new fashion.

Through these interventions in history, God manifests Himself in the Old and New Testaments with features that are absolutely new in comparison to those of the cosmic religions: He is the God of the Covenant, who establishes between one people and Himself a permanent communion. By means of this covenant, He shows Himself faithful: He will never revoke the commitments He has made. God also is a just (in the biblical sense) God: His justice is manifested in the plan He has made. Man's justice will henceforth be defined in relation to God's design: the just man will be the man who enters into the divine meaning of existence, whose life will coincide with the very movement of God's love acting in history and carrying out its design there.

These elements (interventions of God in history, historical design of God) add a completely new dimension to the whole gamut of cosmic religions. To read the Bible is therefore to discover God anew.

Islam is to a certain extent heir to this content of the Old Testament (particularly in its concept of the transcendence of God and His radical distinctness from the world). However, in other respects it represents a regression in terms of the biblical concept of God. As Father Mourabac has clearly pointed out, Islam loses the historical dimension of the biblical God to the degree that the intervention of the Prophet is not the announcement of an eschatological act by God at the end of time, greater than anything He has accomplished in the past ("Remember not former things . . . behold I do new things," said Isaias) but has for its object merely to bring back to its pure state a primitive monotheism constantly on the decline.

Thus, in Islam, time loses the positive dimension it had in Judaism and in Christianity. We are back to a vertical concept of the relationship between man and God. On that score, there is a kind of loss. While retaining from the Bible the concept of a transcendent and holy God, Islam loses the idea of the action of God in history and of God's following of a plan. In any comparative study of religions, therefore, it would have to be situated between Judaism and the cosmic religions, even though, chronologically, it came after both Judaism and Christianity.

3) *The concept of God in Christianity*

The final phase of God's revelation is characterized by the fact that, in Christ, the very intimacy of the life of God, absolutely inaccessible to man's grasp, is unveiled in the mystery of the Three Persons and of the eternal love existing in God from all eternity. Again, there is something radically new here, not only with respect to the cosmic religions, but also to Judaism and to Islam.

Certain trinities found, for example, in Brahmanism or in other religions, are really not on the same level at all as the Christian Trinity. These trinities are always the expression of a radical primeval unity which then is deployed in secondary manifestations which can just as readily be triple, quadruple, etc. Unity is what is first. Multiplicity always appears as a certain degrading of this initial unity.

This corresponds to the spontaneous inclination of the spirit which tends to restore all things to unity. The paradox of the Christian Trinity—which, if we reflect on it, is an amazing paradox—is that the "Three" is just as primitive as the "One." Love is part of the very structure of the being. This is an unbelievable, paradoxical fact whose very consequences are immense. Love, insofar as it is eternal exchange of persons, constitutes that which is the ultimate basis of all existence. It explains that all existence, to be valid, must be the mirror and reflection of this eternal love. Love will be the only way of being in the image of Being.

There is nothing like this in any philosophy or in any religion. An astonishing paradox, too! The mind has trouble bearing it, and it is said that the early Christians themselves had a great deal of difficulty accepting it. They began by trying to interpret it in every way they could, by reducing the object of faith to a more rational concept, in the juxtaposition of the Father, Who is the first God, the Son, Who is inferior to Him, the Spirit, still more inferior—that is, by means of systems which satisfy reason but which are thoroughly heretical and moreover assume the absurd idea of a degrading of the divinity.

Thus, by a strict analysis of the contents of the idea of God, we reach levels of reality which are truly different. To make this all clear is the object of a rigorous objective study of religions.

II. *The paths of access to God*

What do we find at the level of the cosmic religions? Essentially, a "religious experience." The religious experience is a universal fact, by no means a Christian fact. Religious experience, religious sentiment, these are commonly found in all religions. Outside of Christianity we can even find religious experiences of very high quality. There are great religious personalities in Hinduism, in Islamism, in Taoism, and so on, and we can admire them unreservedly. I would even say that it is perfectly possible that at a given moment in the world, the greatest religious personalities may not be Christian. For what is important—and this, too, is one of the ways in which we err—is not the religious genius of a man, but the truth to which he bears witness. "We are not great religious personalities, we are servants of the

Word," Guardini has written. Put another way, we do not bear witness to ourselves, we do not say: "I am a master of religious things," but, "I bear witness to a word which I have received."

At the level of religions, the field of religious experience presents infinite treasures. Heiler, the great historian of religion, has written a book on prayer in all the religions. Prayer is an absolutely universal fact. The liturgical expression of prayer, the sacred act, sacrifice, is also common to all religions. The mystical experience itself is, in one sense, part of the common domain of religions. There is in this order a natural mystique, that is, a certain experience of God which men can attain by turning inward and by an effort of asceticism.

With the man of the Bible, we enter another domain which is no longer that of religious experience, but that of faith. Faith is something absolutely new. There may be men who have faith, but who are not great religious personalities, whose religious experience may be meager. On the other hand, there may be people who possess a great religious genius but do not have faith. This is something which is sometimes disturbing: to meet a highly religious personality, a Hindu, for instance, or a Moslem, who exercises a real fascination. We can respond to this by transposing the saying of Our Lord when He says, regarding John the Baptist, that "he is the greatest of the sons of women, but the least in the Kingdom of the Father is greater than he." That is to say, a small baptized child is greater than the greatest religious geniuses of the cosmic religions, because they are of a totally different order.

What is faith? Essentially, it is adherence to revelation, to the word of God. Faith introduces us into a universe inaccessible to religious experience, into a participation in the life of God and the knowledge of God to which God alone can lead us. Revelation is an act of God. In religion, man seeks God, but God is inaccessible in His innermost being. This is why, in revelation, God comes looking for man, takes him where he is, and raises him up to make him capable, through God's power alone, of attaining what he is incapable of attaining by himself. In this sense, it may be said that revelation achieves the desire of religions, that there is, for the religious man, no better way of being faithful to his religion than to adhere to revelation. This is why conversion to Christianity is never an infidelity for the pagan. This point should be emphasized over and over again. The pagan will keep all the religious values of his paganism, but he will find in Christ the response to all that his desires called for. As St. Paul says, this God for whom he was groping but only through shadows and symbols, this God comes looking for him to give Himself to him, and to reveal to him what He is.

The tragedy of the religions, as Guardini so clearly saw, is wishing to persist once revelation has arrived. This is what Guardini called "the tragedy of the precursor." We may say that there was a time when Buddha was right, and Guardini dares affirm that Buddha was perhaps a great precursor of Christ. That is to say that there was a moment when Buddha, through his experience, in his natural mysticism, interpreted that which was accessible of God through His revelation in the world. But from the moment when this God whom Buddha was seeking manifested Himself, the precursor, whose very mission was to prepare, had to efface himself. This is why Guardini says that Buddha was perhaps a great precursor of Christ, and that he will unquestionably be His final enemy. There is a moment when the precursor becomes the enemy. Thus it was when the Old Testament, which was preparing for Christ, became Judaism, opposed to Christ. Something which has been true can become false, at the precise moment when it becomes outdated. In this regard, the criterion in the comparison of religions, is the historical criterion.

Religions correspond essentially to successive moments in the revelation of God, and what is demanded of man, as St. Ireneus put it, is to avoid remaining in his infancy when the age for being an adult has arrived. "You had the Law, which was made for children who had need of being ruled from without; today you are called to the liberty of the sons of God. Why do you remain in the chains of the Law, which was destined only to provide your up-bringing but which, from the moment you were called to become free men, ceases to have any value?"

When a man wants to remain too attached to his youth and does not succeed in detaching himself from it, this youth somehow poisons him. In this sense, a man's childhood can be an excessive burden and its encumbrances can prevent him from fulfilling himself. So it is for the history of mankind. We might say that, for mankind, paganism is the fact of wanting to remain in infancy, of thereby failing to accept the new revelation that would make it an adult, the revelation given first in the Old Testament and then in Christ.

III. *The vision of time and history*

The attitude toward the mystery of time represents one of the aspects under which the discernment of religions best manifests itself. The opposition here is that of the myth and of eschatology.

The chief feature of the cosmic religions, from this point of view, is indeed the myth. In the history of religions, a major part of the works on the pagan religions is devoted to myths. Myths are the theology of the cosmic religions. They are chiefly cosmological myths which, in a world preceding time, relate the accomplishment by the gods of all the realities which subsequently are to be unfolded and manifested through the ages.

The man of the cosmic religions thinks that all things were initially accomplished in a former world, which is the world of myths (as Van der Leeuw, in particular, brought out) and that the purpose of rituals is essentially to renew on a perpetual basis, by means of a kind of imitation of the pre-existing acts of the gods, the forces of the life constantly threatened with degradation. In other words, we have here a pessimistic concept of time. Time is dispersion, degradation; one must fight against this destructive action of time by maintaining contact with the original. The ritual is therefore the link established between the present moment and the original reality. Illustrations of this can be found in all the cosmic religions: in particular, these are the beginning-of-the-year ritual, or the rites for the different seasons, the rites of the harvest, the grape-gathering, and so on. In the African religions, as well as in the religions of ancient Greece (the religions of Eleusis, for instance, which were essentially religions of fertility), or in the religions of India, these rites translate a fundamental idea, that of the life of the cosmos, of its cyclical renewal, which must find its sources in the original world of pre-existing myths.

On the other hand, the biblical attitude toward time places the stress on the future. With Isaias and the biblical man, creation is a future far more than a past. Paradise is a future. The great works of God are rather expected in the future than accomplished in the past. There is a reversal of attitudes. Man's behavior is no longer based on experience, but on faith, that is, on promise. And the basis of hope —the biblical man is essentially the man of hope—is the fidelity of God to His promise. Relying on this promise, man can face time with the certitude that, despite all the apparent contradictions, the promises of God regarding life after death will some day be fulfilled.

And so it is that we can much better understand the saying which appears four times in Isaias, like the hinge of the Bible: "Remember not former things . . . Behold I do new things . . . I will make a way in the wilderness, and rivers in the desert" (an allusion to the crossing of the Red Sea). Otherwise stated, the new exodus, the new Passover, the liberation effected at the end of time, will be infinitely greater than the former Passover; the great works of God in the future will overshadow the great works of God in the past, regardless of how great these works may have been. This is why the Bible is essentially *prophecy*; prophecy is fundamentally a biblical characteristic.

At once, time is given value. No longer is it a degraded version of a perfect and unchanging eternity. It is the arena of God's design. Time is that in which the magnificent work whose accomplishment God has promised is progressively carried out. We may contrast the man of the myth and the man of the Bible with two examples. The man of the myth is essentially Ulysses—and we must not forget that his poems (the *Odyssey*) are called *Nostoi* in Greek, that is, the returns (the same word from which "nostalgia" is derived, for nostalgia is the suffering of return, the desire to return to the beginning). Ulysses, after leaving Ithaca and after having sailed around the Mediterranean, returns to his point of departure. This is the very image of cyclical time, of time which turns on its own axis, which perpetually comes back to its origin, but which in the end has no direction, ends nowhere and goes nowhere, and remains turned toward the past. This nostalgia for the beginning is found also in the poets, in the nostalgia for the paradise lost of childhood. Poetry, says Rilke, consists merely in removing "fragments of childhood from the destructive action of time."

Contrasted with Ulysses is Abraham. Abraham leaves Ur of the Chaldees, but he is never to return. He leaves Ur relying on the promise of God that He will give him the land of promise, and, confident in this promise, he enters into the adventure of time with all its unknowns; he leaves the world of experience, the world of the known, and moves toward the unknown relying only on faith. The Epistle to the Hebrews says of Abraham: "he left not knowing where he was going." Gregory of Nyssa states that this ignorance proves that he was on the right path, for he was relying on the only word capable of introducing him to the new world. As the Protestant professor Jean Hériny has written, in a very beautiful phrase, "the model of the pagan is the princess sent into exile who dreams of returning; *the model of the Christian is Abraham who sets out on the road toward an unknown land that God will show him.*" The biblical attitude demands that nostalgia be overcome. This dialogue between the pagan soul and the biblical soul goes on in each of us; the temptation to regret the past struggles against the courage to face the future. Thus we see that the prophetic attitude is a victory over the pagan inclination which persists in every man. This kind of victory is not possible without the intervention of a new element, the word, the promise, the rock on which we may rely.

Once again we end up with a phenomenology which brings to the fore two attitudes. The second of them in no way takes away any of the riches of the first, but it does give rise to an element which goes beyond it. It is, moreover, wonderful to see, particularly in the liturgy, how the Mosaic religion, and then the Christian religion, follow from the cosmic religions and finally assimilate it.

One last example demonstrates that there is really a continuity made up of successive enrichment and not of opposition. The feast of Passover was at the outset the seasonal feast of the first grain. One outstanding trace of this remains, the use of the unleavened bread, which is directly related to the making of the first loaves with the new grain, when there is no more leaven, the leaven being the old flour; and this, consequently, connects us with a cosmic, pre-Mosaic, pre-Biblical stratum of religion. Within the framework of this seasonal feast the Jewish Passover came to be inserted, to celebrate the departure from Egypt. Finally, Christ Our Lord rose again within the framework of this same Passover, inscribing this new instance of the interventions of God in the very history of the former interventions, thereby demonstrating that He had not come to destroy but to fulfill. This we must understand even of the pagan religions. In this regard, do we not invoke in the liturgy of the Mass, before the sacrifice of Christ, the sacrifice of Abel and the sacrifice of Melchisedech, which derive from cosmic religion, and the sacrifice of Abraham which derives from the Mosaic religion, thus indicating that the sacrifice of Christ is interpolated in the succession of the other sacrifices, that it simply marks their fulfillment, accomplishing in its fullness the reality of Sacrifice?

2. ANDRE RETIF, S.J.

THE RELIGIONS OF NATURE

At the outset, it would be well to put aside the term "religions of primitives" to designate the religions of peoples who have remained close to nature. For, as a matter of fact, they have a long history of civilization.

Then we must stress the importance of the way of life and of the cultural environment in determining religious practices. Essentially, we shall distinguish the gatherer-hunters, the specialized hunters, the farmers, and the shepherds.

Among the "gatherer-hunters," such as the Pygmies, the women do the gathering while the men hunt small game with simple methods. This form of civilization is centered on the monogamous home, more out of necessity than out of moral or religious principle.

Among the "hunters," the economy is founded on systematic and organized hunting, and the technical methods are completely different, being marked by the importance of the solar and seasonal myths and by the cult of the founder-hero.

Since we cannot go into detail, we must of necessity limit ourselves here to the common or at least general features of specialized and perfected. This presupposes a more advanced social organization, and the chief of the clan is also the religious chief.

Among the "farmers," the woman plays a fundamental role. Remaining in the home while the husband was hunting, she must have had the leisure to observe the growth of plants and so discovered agriculture. The civilization became oriented in a matriarchal sense, attributing the greater importance to the lineage of the women.

Among the nomad "shepherds," the religious character is these very diverse religious attitudes. Despite the heterogeneity of religious structures, there are some points found everywhere or almost everywhere.

Then, we shall go into greater depth concerning the religion of the farmers.

One of the essential cultural characteristics is the *awareness of identification with a reality endowed with vital powers*. This reality may be:

1) *An animal*—this is totemism. Thus, the tribe of the serpent is forbidden to kill a serpent because, for the African, there is an identification between man and a given animal called the "alter ego animal." Killing a serpent would cause the death of the tribal chieftain. From such beliefs spring very rigid taboos and severe penalties for those who violate the prohibitions. Thus, numerous tribes have a family tie with an animal which becomes sacred and the depository of the tribe's soul.

2) *A spirit,* the soul's double, enjoying very considerable freedom and independence. For this reason, these people do not like to be awakened suddenly, for fear that their double, which may leave their body during sleep, may not have time to re-enter them.

Lévy-Bruhl points out the numerous moral consequences of this participation. He relates that a Negro, having dreamed that a white man had stolen fruit from his garden during the night, accused him of it. The European proved that on that very night, he had been over 100 miles away. For him, it was clear—he could not have stolen. But for the African, the dream was real; it was the white's double who had stolen. That was no less certain. There was no contradiction between the theft and the absence of the white man, but rather a juxtaposition of two realities which it would be impossible to reconcile.

3) *A group.* The awareness of belonging to a group is very strong in these people. The group is considered as a living body and, just as a member cannot live without being attached to the body, so too a member of the group cannot live outside this group. This feeling of participating in a collectivity, in a community of which one is a member, underlies all sorts of attitudes found among these primitive and traditional populations. To cut someone off from this vital source is to condemn him to death.

These cultural types have often been referred to as pre-logical. Let us humbly recognize that our own mentality remains marked with certain feelings of fear, of sentimentality, which are no more logical.

Animism, in the full sense of the word, "cult of spirits," is found only in a rural environment. Let us examine more closely the religious mentality of these agrarian communities. They believe in two kinds of invisible beings: the spirits and the dead.

The *spirits* are ambiguous beings, neither essentially good nor essentially evil. The only thing that counts is their attitude toward man, the manifestation of their presence and of their power, either beneficent or malevolent depending on the circumstances. From this there follows a pragmatic attitude on the part of the African who will avoid putting himself in a bad light with respect to these spirits by crossing them. The sorcerers, the soothsayers, the priests, are specialists in relations with the spirits.

In this aspect of invisible spirits dwelling in stones, trees, springs, we find again the idea of the presence of a vital force, as Tempels pointed out so well in *The Bantu Philosophy* (Col. Présence Afric.).

For this sedentary type, there exists, beyond the familiar world of his house, his market-place, his village, a whole unknown world peopled with redoubtable beings which begins where the familiar world ends: the forest, the mountain, things which the hunter does not fear. The African locates his cemeteries on the borders of this unknown world. In Madagascar, where clan cemeteries do not exist, the dead of a family are buried along the edges of the family field.

The dead continue to be a part of the community of the living. And the greatest misfortune is not to be buried in the family burial-ground. Renouncing this was a very difficult form of detachment for the first priestly vocations in Africa. During the war, the Madagascar soldiers would bring back to the families of their comrades killed in combat a few bones, some hair, so that the burial could be carried out. If a man drowns or is eaten by a shark, a search will be made until some part of him has been found.

Belief in the survival of souls seems to be coupled with a persistent fear that the dead are not satisfied with their new existence and that they may "return" to manifest their discontent. In addition, funeral rites are always scrupulously observed. In Madagascar, the body is borne to the grave on a zig-zag course so that the dead person may not find his way back to the house. Manifestations of boisterous gaiety alternate with moans and rending screams; on the one hand, it is necessary to accompany the deceased with singing and dancing so that he or she may enjoy the passage to the grave and so that the new existence may appear in a favorable light; and on the other hand, to abstain from spectacular lamentations would be to scorn tradition, to lack respect for the departed one, to provoke the wrath of the invisible ones.

The "return of the dead" consists in exhuming the cadavers from the grave after several years and wrapping them in a "lambamena" (shroud); men carry the corpse on a pole, parading it through the town while they dance, followed by musicians and the family, who also dance. This ceremony is a very joyous feast accompanied by banquets. It lasts several days.

From the cult of the dead, or *manism*, comes the *respect for idealized ancestors*, to the point that it is the ancestors who rule, the living chief being but the representative of the founder of the tribe. Christianity must therefore not be presented to these people as being against ancestors. St. Francis Xavier used to answer the first Christians of Japan who questioned him about the fate of their ancestors by saying that they had little chance of being saved. Let us not imitate him on this point, but let us rather say: "Since your ancestors wanted to do the right thing and knew God in their own way, you may hope to see them again in Paradise. If they were alive today, they would become Christians just as they would light their houses with electricity instead of candles."

Additional forms of animism

Masks are used throughout the animist world, with numerous nuances: The mask might simply represent a god or supernatural personage, without itself possessing any spiritual or magical substance. Or the spirit itself, or some magical power emanating from it, might be thought to dwell in the mask, making it dangerous for the profane. Thus, the anti-feminine societies which arise in matriarchies, use masks to frighten the women—the men make them think that the sight of the mask will bring them misfortune.

The *fetish*, closely related to the masks, is a sacred object which is believed to enclose a spirit shut in at the mercy of men. This fetish does not only represent God, it is the support of the divine presence. If the fetish ceases acting, it is thought that the spirit has escaped it and the object loses all value. There are fetishes that women must not look upon. The fact of selling them to a stranger, especially to a white man, causes the spirit to leave. Sometimes the African, believing that a spirit is dwelling in a tree in the forest, cuts it down and brings it home.

The fetish is distinguished from the good-luck talisman by the idea that is formed of its efficacy—the talisman is only credited with a non-personalized magical power.

Magic is part of animism: man captures the power of the god and forces it to do what he wants. This rabid anthropocentrism is the very opposite of religion. Constraining God by his actions, his words, man seems stronger than He. On the contrary, in religion, man prays, but the final decision is God's; God is stronger than man.

Cosmobiology and mystery

The animist sees the world as a multiplicity of living things: every reality which produces some kind of effect, whether psychological or material, is thought to be moved by an immanent presence. He conceives of himself as being integrated into a whole whose equilibrium is uncertain and may be destroyed. Because man is part of a cosmic whole made up of multiple solidarities, the fact that he may break certain moral laws can have repercussions throughout the entire world.

In order to understand this unitary vision represented by cosmobiology, it is necessary to get back to the agrarian environment, for it is the spiritual expression of the latter and at the very root of the agrarian complex: the invention and consequent administration of the cultivation of plants by the woman who thereby took on a very great importance in primitive societies. The fertility of the earth was linked with female fertility: soil sown by a woman, a harvest reaped by a woman, will be better than if the work has been done by a man. There is not only a relationship, but internal parallelism between the biological cycles of the woman and the biological cycles of the earth and of vegetation, between the cycle of the woman and the cycle of the moon. And so the entire mystery of the universe is linked with the mystery of the woman.

This kind of view of things led man to experience anxiety, fear of woman. In the matriarchal societies, he felt himself in danger of having only an accessory role (thus the boy does not inherit from his father but from the brother of his mother—his uncle is his tutor). Considering himself as secondary, the man has tried to react against domination by the woman, and everywhere in agrarian groups secret societies of men, of a clearly anti-feminine nature, have appeared. This obsession concerning the woman goes as far as complexes of a psychoanalytical order and vices against nature.

The *agrarian rites* have as their purpose re-establishing the cosmological equilibrium of the world. Mimes of ancient legends and myths accompany every crisis: change of seasons, of the moon, critical moments for vegetation, for human life. These are times when the feeling of solidarity of all things and all men, of nature and man, is in full play. Man wants to strengthen the movement of nature by a greater biological activity. The men dance when a woman is lying-in, so that she may have more vital force. Sacrifices, dances, ritual meals run all through the seasonal phenomena. The same holds true at births, weddings, deaths, and especially at the moment when children pass into adulthood. While the initiations vary according to the civilizations, they always consist in an intense period of life during which the child will symbolically die and be re-born. The child is subjected to difficult trials: whipping till the blood flows, fasting, ant stings, painting of the body, and so on. Then he is initiated into the laws of the tribe. He receives a new name. After this, the adolescent must act as though he were re-born. Having forgotten everything from the past, he learns once more to speak, to eat, to walk, just like a new baby. Until the initiation, the boys do what they want while the girls work hard. After the initiation, the boys, having become responsible persons, must obey their ancestors.

To this psychological aspiration of "passage" to a higher reality of existence, the Bible and Christianity will contribute the true passage of the Lord's "Passover," realized in Jesus Christ in His Church with her worship and her sacraments, particularly Baptism and Confirmation. (cf. Encyclical *Princeps Pastorum* of John XXIII).

The notion of *myths* which represent and explain the origin of things remains to be developed. Let us simply say that we find here again the female biology: Earth—Mother—Moon, and close this brief sketch of the nature religions by seeking to define the notion of God which they include.

The notion of God varies greatly depending on the types of civilizations.

In the sedentary world of the rural peoples, the notion of a God, the Supreme Being, is found everywhere. But this God is more often than not a being too far removed to be accessible. It is a question more of deism than of theism.[1]

This Supreme Being is generally considered as creator and proprietor of all creation. He remains far off and therefore hardly dangerous, and He is not tendered any clear or well-formulated worship. In fact, because God is good, He can do no evil. It is not necessary to concern oneself about Him. On the contrary, the worship will be directed instead to the spirits and the dead whom man must conciliate, for they could be harmful to him. Still, in the majority of sacrifices and initiations, the name of God is mentioned. In Madagascar, it recurs constantly in the word *Zanahary*. And the prayers addressed to Him are not only requests, but also acts of thanksgiving. The forms of this worship of the Supreme Being have long gone unnoticed, because they are most often individual and escape the notice of researchers. But some fine observers have noted numerous actions which can only be explained by some relation to God. In *Religious Formation in Black Africa* Father Van Bulck cites some examples of this:

"In the Belgian Congo, early in the morning, while the entire village is still sleeping, a mother stands behind her hut, raises her newborn child to heaven, presenting him thus

[1] By theism is understood a belief in a God who efficaciously and intimately influences daily life, a belief on which man centers active religious, moral and cultural preoccupations. (e.g. Civilization of the "gatherers and shepherds".) Deism, on the other hand, is a concept of a theoretical and abstract God. (cf. Voltaire and the watchmaker of the world.)

to the Supreme Being. At the same time, her lips mumble a short prayer of offering or of filial request. . . .

"On another day, one of the sons of the family must go on a long trip. At the very moment he leaves the paternal roof, his father invokes the protection of Heaven in order to guarantee his safe return. . . .

"A conference has begun, or even just a rather lively discussion. A man makes a simple gesture with his hand; all those who are conversant with the customs immediately understand that he is taking the Supreme Being as witness of the sincerity of the words he is going to utter."

Nevertheless, the references to God are everywhere rarer than the references to the spirits.

Missionary conclusion

These civilizations of nature baffle us a little. However, they represent a religious type of great value which must be absorbed into the Christianity of these peoples. A few examples will show how conversion to Christianity will complete this religious drive:

The innate sense of *community* will have to be transposed into the notion of the Mystical Body, which these African societies are far more likely to understand than we. Starting with the idea that man cannot live outside the community, the missionary will be able to explain that the Christian life is not possible outside the Church, for the Church is the maternal bosom, the vital source, of every Christian; outside of her, there is death. He may compare the Church to a supernatural clan in which (and this is not always the case in natural clans) each one's personality is highly respected.

The notion of *sacrifice* is also transferable. The Africans already have a deep understanding of it. It is the gift or surrender to a superior power of an animal which, being killed and offered up, becomes sacred. It often ends with communion, in which man assimilates part of the sacred energy incorporated in the sacrificed object. One can imagine the fulfillment and sublimation that would be contributed to these beliefs by the correct notion of the Redemption and the Eucharist, vital sacrifice *par excellence*, ontological transmission of God's power.

The *solidarity of man with the cosmos* is something very beautiful which we in the West have lost too completely from view. Characteristic of the thinking of Father Teilhard de Chardin, it renders this thinking well adapted to an African mentality. And we can re-learn from the Africans that solidarity with nature which is part of Christianity (cf. St. Paul).

It is therefore with great respect and sympathy that we must approach these traditional religious structures, without minimizing the deviations and the gaps which Christianity must correct or fill up. We must pray that the evangelization of these peoples will be accomplished in depth, preserving what is good in their traditions: the more Christianity in a country becomes "indigenous," the more profoundly is that country Christianized. It would be inappropriate and vain to wish to Christianize a country without straining Christianity through that country's own philosophy, without giving it a local coloration. The work of Christianization and that of the "indigenization" of Christianity must therefore be carried on together.

3. JOSEPH HOURS, S.J. | ISLAM

It is impossible to speak of Islam adequately without participating in it from the inside. Islam is, at one and the same time, a religious, social, political and economic reality which refuses to make any distinction among these points of view. Lacking a presentation from the inside, therefore, Islam must always be placed in its own environment and in its historical development. The Moslem dogma makes sense only in this context.

I shall accordingly try to present Islam in its historical development, following three major divisions: presentation of Mohammed and the Koran; phase of expansion of Islam which coincides with the effort to establish the Moslem community; and finally, the modern era, which will give us points of contact between Islam and today's world, and therefore with us Christians.

I. *The life of Mohammed*

What do we know of Mohammed? Nothing very precise in the historical sense of the word. There are many lives of Mohammed, but they were published belatedly, the first nearly 150 years after his death. Born around 570 A.D., into a noble family of Mecca of the tribe of Quraysh, he was orphaned at an early age and was raised by one of his uncles. While still very young, he entered the service of a rich widow, Khadija, whose fortune was largely in the caravan trade which operated along the coast of Arabia, joining the Orient and the Mediterranean. Mecca, a center for pilgrimages, was also a great caravan center.

This widow became fond of Mohammed and married him. His social situation was thereby transformed. It was then that his religious crisis began. On several occasions, he took refuge in the deserts around Mecca where he received what may be called his "calling"; this is traditionally placed around the year 612. The lives of Mohammed relate that he saw a supernatural being which told him to preach. There are variations in the accounts of this vision; the essential point is that, at the beginning of Mohammed's life, there was a phenomenon of a purely religious order, a call coming from God. The first *Suras** of the Koran bear witness to this consciousness on the part of Mohammed of having been called.

Following this first call, Mohammed, encouraged by Khadija, began to preach before small groups of acquaintances rather than in front of the public at large. Then, he recruited a small nucleus of disciples who formed the basis of Islam, such as the old Abu-Bakr, Omar and his cousin Ali. Now he became bolder and went out to preach to the Meccans, but very soon he encountered persecution.

The persecution was initially expressed in harassment. Why was this? First of all, he was reprimanded for disturbing the public order, for being a bit bizarre. But very soon, since Mohammed's essential affirmation was monotheism and Mecca was an important pilgrimage center, the new religion seemed to be in conflict with the traditional religion

---

* (T.N. The term "Sura" as used in the Koran may mean either a complete chapter, or part of a chapter, or may even have the sense of *revelation.*)

of Mecca. The opposition seems not to have been directed solely to the dogmatic level. Paganism was undoubtedly not very vigorous at that time in Mecca.

Mohammed put up with these annoyances so long as he was able to have the protection of his clan. His uncle continued to have confidence in him. And in a tribal civilization, the clan holds an important place, so that whoever attacks one member of the clan attacks the entire clan.

But then, there came the year of mourning with the death of his uncle and of Khadija. Now, everything changed. His opponents in Mecca obtained his exclusion from the clan. Mohammed, alone now, had to resolve this dilemma: either to say what he had to say, which could lead even to martyrdom, or to leave that place and go find a more favorable location, with the option of returning some day. This was the fundamental choice. Islam is not mistaken when it traces its origins to that moment of Mohammed's departure for Medina. It is an important phenomenon in understanding Islam. "The blood of martyrs is the seed of Christians"—Mohammed does not appear to have realized that for ideas to triumph, it is not necessary that their propagators survive. Because he did not die for his ideas, Mohammed would soon have to impose them, by force if necessary.

He tried first to leave for Tâ'if, was expelled, then sent his followers into Ethiopia to the Negus, who received them as Christians. He entered into contact with some inhabitants of a neighboring oasis, Yathrib, and left for there. Yathrib subsequently became Medina, the "city of the prophet" (Madinat al Nabi).

The beginnings in Medina were difficult. He had been summoned there as an arbiter, there being a precarious peace among the diverse elements of a mixed population consisting of two Arab tribes, the Aws and the Khazraj, and three Jewish tribes, the Nadir, the Qaynoja and the Qorayza. Being in the minority, weakened by an internal war, the Arabs had felt the need of selecting a chief who could reunite them and hold his own against the Jews who were threatening to annex them. Mohammed made a kind of pact establishing equality. To each his own religion; they were all to try to leave in peace. They would all take part equally in military expeditions. He tried to keep the friendship of both sides. For a period of time, he fixed, for prayers, the same direction as the Jews, Jerusalem, and imposed a fast similar to that of the Jews (*kippur*).

But people had to live; a very simple means of doing so was the raid, and this won Mohammed the prestige of a military chieftain. The first raids, however, were not very hazardous. When he felt more sure of himself, Mohammed turned on the Meccans, his former compatriots. The break came when he attacked them during a sacred truce near the oasis of Nakhla. At the same time, Islam marked its originality by detaching itself from the Jewish environment and turning toward Mecca for prayer, thereby changing the orientation of the qibla. This took place around 623.

Mecca represented a more considerable force than the nascent Islam. The first contacts were defensive, with alternating successes and defeats. Mohammed won a first victory in a skirmish near the well of Badr. Then he was defeated at Mount 'Ohod. Finally, the definitive battle of "The Ditch" enabled him to remove the Meccan pressure.

At the same time, by a delicate balancing act, Mohammed was evicting the Jews from Medina. In three years, he succeeded in conquering the Meccans and chasing the Jews from the oasis.

The year 627 was a turning-point. Mohammed inaugurated an expansion phase by signing a peace treaty on an equal footing with Mecca in 628 (at Hudaybiyya). He now became a power in Arabia. He died triumphant, in 632.

It is difficult to form a very clear idea of the physiognomy of this man. This is a very rich and complex personality, difficult to know. The private man is unquestionably the least sympathetic: harem life, assassination used as a means of political pressure. Other traits are more attractive, such as the love of the grandfather for his grandchildren, something which is quite characteristic of the Moslem sentiment.

The political man is remarkable. To him is due the unification of Arabia and the creation of a real power center at the juncture of Ethiopia, Persia and Byzantium.

As a man of war, he also reveals a strong personality. He took part in 27 expeditions, and received many wounds.

Finally, Mohammed may be considered as a legislator; to him we owe the birth of the Moslem code.

But what stands out above all, is the aspect of the religious man, with his mystical as well as prophetic side. The first *Sura* attest to a real and direct contact with God. The tone of certain revelations, the subjects dealt with, are also proof of this. (Of course the term "prophet" as applied to Mohammed must not be taken in the Old Testament sense.)

The Koran

The Koran left by Mohammed is the basis of Islam, the source of information for the religious conscience of the majority of Moslems. General Randot, in *Islam and Today's Moslems*, gives us a good picture of those old men, otherwise uncultured, who have as their sole training the Koran, reread and meditated on at length.

The book is divided into verses, about 6,600 of them, with variations according to the version. It is composed of a collection of the different sermons of Mohammed brought together by his disciples and transmitted by oral tradition. Partial collections were rather quickly put together. Caliph Othman, around 650, had everything which existed of Mohammed's sermons brought together, suppressing the variations. The establishment of the critical text is of no special interest (150 variations instead of 2,000 in the case of the New Testament).

The problem of repetitions, which is normal in partial collections, did not arise. There is no logical order, but this is of no consequence.

Nevertheless, the revelations of the beginning (Mecca), more religious, centering on the last ends, were rather quickly distinguished from the revelations of the end (Medina), which are more juridical (internal organization of the Moslem community). That is readily understandable; at the end of his life, Mohammed was not addressing members whom he had to convert, but faithful whom he had to organize.

When one reads the Koran, one is struck by the reminders of the Old Testament, and every Westerner asks himself about the sources of the Koran. This problem does not exist for the Moslems, since the revelations come directly from God. Revelation is contained in a celestial archetype which God has revealed generation after generation. It was found that men have not been able to keep this divine revelation faithfully. Some knowingly misrepresented it: these are the Jews; the others did so out of ignorance: they are the Christians. Nevertheless, both Jews and Christians retain features of the primordial Revelation. Mohammed has come to re-establish the truth. It is not to be wondered at that common traits are to be found in the Koran, the Old Testament and the New Testament. But the Koran stamps as authentic the preceding Scriptures, just as Mohammed places his seal on the prophets who followed one another before him.

For the Western mind, there is a problem here and it remains unsolved. This problem is interesting from the scientific point of view, but has no bearing on the understanding of present-day Islam.

Rather than summing up the Koran, it would be better to attempt a synthetic presentation of the Koranic universe. It includes various personages: God known under the name of Allah, or the names of His attributes, unity, omnipotence, and so on. Underneath, the supernatural beings, angels, demons, djinns. Then, some scarcely definable beings, abstract entities analogous to the eons of Greek philosophy, which accompany God's action: truth, word, order, spirit. These entities beget one another. Below them, the prophets (Mohammed, the Biblical and non-Biblical prophets). Finally, men.

These personages are distributed along a time scale which includes: the beginning (creation), the past which preceded Mohammed, the present, the era of Mohammed and of Islam, the end of the world, and the next world. Past and present are very near, end and beyond as well. In short, there is a kind of triptych: beginning, present, beyond. No future.

During this time, the drama of the Koran, the salvation of man, unfolds. While at first glance the Koran seems to proclaim the omnipotence of God, in fact it is an anthropocentric book. Man appears therein as the center of the universe.

The revelation and legislation of the Koran have a human goal. What is revealed is not the inner life of God, but that which is necessary for man. The rewards, hell, paradise, are also for man. The Moslem paradise involves only men. There is nothing about a beatific vision, nothing about coming face to face with God. Whether one deals with the past, the present, the beyond, it is essentially a matter of something human.

The differences with Christianity, whose drama is primarily Christocentric, are fundamental. It is necessary for the Christian to know the divine life incarnated in man. But Islam does not recognize the Incarnation.

Man, who is the center of the Koran, first of all appears in a neutral state, a natural state: biological, intelligent, affective, capable of morality. But very soon he is polarized either toward good or evil; thus humanity is divided into good and bad people, into believers, the *muminun*, and the godless, the *kafirun*. This separation between good and bad people takes place both in the present and the beyond. In the present, this is done by the revelation and the attitude of faith or rejection adopted toward it by men. Once he has chosen one category or the other, man stays in it. The attitude of God is therefore polarized; His behavior is ruled by the division of mankind. If God addresses Himself to the good people, He will enlighten them to lead them to Paradise. If He addresses Himself to the wicked, He will harden their hearts and blind them, or, as the Koran says, "place an envelope over their hearts to prevent them from understanding and a covering over their eyes to prevent them from seeing." There is predestination. The conflict between divine power and human liberty crops up very soon. Historically, this problem arose for Mohammed from the outset of the Hegira. He is persuaded that he has the light. God has given him the revelation. If God sends the revelation, and God is all-powerful, then men must believe. But they do not believe; therefore, it must be that God does not want them to believe. And when Mohammed speaks, the others do not understand, for if they did understand, they would believe.

This conflict between human freedom and God's omnipotence is expressed in the Koran in a rudimentary state. Mohammed simultaneously affirms that man is free in his actions and that God is all-powerful. It is difficult to know what concept Mohammed had originally regarding human freedom. The most accurate approximation we can make is that for him, man is responsible for the good and the evil which he does by himself. However, this does not mean that he is free. Man is ruled when he chooses his attitude toward revelation, and later in the chosen path.

This is an important consequence for the present time. The basic difficulty Islam experiences in considering non-Moslems on an equal footing has its source in a truth, a theological truth, as far as it is concerned. Islam is the truth, and truth has a right to exist. Truth is always superior to error; Islam must therefore be superior to the rest of the world. It is all perfectly logical.

Another conclusion: man lives in a revealed universe in which everything is given him from the outside. There is no distinction between the natural order and the supernatural order. There is no natural morality based on reason. Everything comes from God. This is very different from our Christian notion of revelation.

This was the heritage of the Moslem community at the death of Mohammed in 632.

II. *The Extension of Islam*

After some difficult times, Islam organized itself and set out to conquer the world. An important fact: it is at the moment Islam became aware of itself as a material force that it began to develop as a politico-religious community, and that the Moslem theology began to be formulated on the basis of the Koran.

The conquest was swift. Syria fell between 634 and 636, Alexandria and Egypt in 642. To the north and east, Iraq and Persia fell in 642, at Qadisiya, where the last of the Sassanides was beaten, at the same time as the capture of Alexandria. Spain was conquered at the same time as Central Asia. In 714, expansion into Turkestan, and in 732, as far as Poitiers.

At the same time as it was being organized as a power, the doctrine was being elaborated; there was always a relationship between political questions and religious questions.

The first question that arose was that of the succession to the prophet. From this came the various schisms, more political than dogmatic, which tore Islam apart.

The first opponents, the Kharijites, maintained that the Caliphate must be subject to God's judgment; the choice of the Caliph does not depend on his origin—he must be the best. Others, the Shiites, affirmed that the successor of Mohammed could be found only in his family (today, Shiism is the national religion in Iran). Kharijites and Shiites would later separate from the orthodox Islam, called Sunnite, for which it suffices that the Caliph be of the tribe of Quraysh.

Islam, then, was established as a community on the administrative level. Toward 696, the Caliph Abd el Malek succeeded in making Arabic the administrative language, and in issuing his first gold currency, marking his economic independence of the Byzantines and the Persians.

On the social level, the question of fiscal problems arose at the outset. Taxes were different for the Moslems and the Christians; the Moslems were subject to legal alms-giving, the Christians were at a disadvantage. One of the Ommeyads, Omar II, carried out a fiscal reform which formed the basis of the Moslem community.

As a religious community, it was at this time that the great Moslem practices were fixed, the establishment of the religious Islam resting on the five great pillars: profession of faith, prayer, almsgiving, Ramadan, pilgrimage. These practices already had their beginnings in the Koran, but it seems that they were not crystallized in the form in which we know them until the 8th century.

Only the profession of faith, or *shahada*, is indispensable for the good Moslem.

Prayer, the *salât*, is essentially ritualistic. Individual prayer is left to the discretion of the believer. Ritual prayer involves ablutions and set times. The prayer at noon on Friday is a community exercise.

The legal alms, the *zakat*, is fixed at 1/5 or 1/10 of one's income. Its meaning is specified in the Koran: it is a loan to God who will repay it in the next world, or else a purification of the goods of this world. It therefore has a very different meaning from our Christian charity, both in its purpose and in its significance.

Ramadan is nothing more than the old Semitic fast. It consists in spending a lunar month without food in the daytime in remembrance of the anniversary of the revelation of the Koran. It ends in a very popular feast in Islam, the *fitr* or *aid el çaghir*, that is, the "little feast."

The pilgrimage, of pre-Islamic origin, was connected by Mohammed with Abraham's memory. One must take part in certain rites: becoming purified by means of a suitable posture, walking around the *ka'ba*, ritual races, stations, stone-throwing, and, in conclusion, sacrifice and de-sacralization.

Moslem theology

Moslem theology was instituted on the basis of political realities. The Koran left two points uncertain: that of human liberty and that of the nature of God, of whom all that is known is that He is, that He is one and all-powerful.

Conflicts having arisen, the theology developed on these two points.

Under the Omeyyads a quarrel arose on the matter of man's freedom. Caliphs without virtue were then at the head of Islam. How was this possible? Some said, God had willed it. Their opponents replied, that is too simple. Whence two tendencies arose: those upholding the freedom of man, the Gadarites, and those upholding the omnipotence of God, the Jabarites. The middle position prevailed, that of the Moujirites who left it up to God—"the believer may be a sinner, but he will never be able to be a great sinner, because he is a believer."

The conflict regarding God and His attributes was born of the confrontation between Islam and Greek philosophy.

God was known by the Moslems by His name, Allah, and by His attributes. What are these attributes? Are they part of the divine essence or are they separate? Are they not so many separate gods? Does this not approach polytheism, something which Islam had wanted to escape? But if, in order to avoid this potential polytheism, the divine essence and its attributes are confused, what is the Koran? The Koran is the word of God; and the word is an attribute of God. But, on the other hand, the Koran is outside God. It is therefore not an attribute of God and cannot be confused with the divine essence. The Koran is therefore not uncreated, as God is, which is contrary to the orthodox theology of Islam, in which both God and the Koran are uncreated.

At first, the Mu'tazilites triumphed, with Caliph al Ma'mûn. It was proclaimed that the Koran was created and that reason could play a part in the development of faith.

Then the wind changed and the adversaries carried the day, with the Ash'arites and Caliph Mutawakkil, who imposed the current theology of Islam. The divine mystery is inaccessible, hidden to human reason. The divine attributes have a reality of their own, but they are not separate from God. The Koran, word of God, is uncreated, like God Himself. The attempt at personal reflection in Moslem theology terminated at this time (850-860). This was of considerable importance for the further development of Moslem dogma. After this time, men were content to comment, with no attempt at discovery. From this stems the struggle of modern reformers to re-open this door of personal effort. All the great names of orthodox Moslem theology belong to this school.

There is, in the Moslem religion, parallel to dogmatic theology, a theology of practice (cf. collections of laws, of jurisprudence). This practical religion, whence develops the popular Moslem conscience, became crystallized in four schools between the end of the 8th and the end of the 9th centuries:

the Malekites (North Africa—death of Malik in 795)
the Hanifites (Turkey—death of Abu Hanifa in 767)
the Shafi'ites (Egypt—death of al Shafi'i in 820)
the Hanbalites (Damascus, Saudi Arabia—death of ibn Hanbal in 855).

Doctrines in these schools vary according to the role assigned to personal interpretation, to judgment by analogy, or to the general opinion of the community.

Islam was therefore established by the 10th century. After this came the dispersion: since Central Asia, Iran, North Africa and Spain got away from the center of power, Islam in those places took on different coloration on the religious level according to the local sub-stratum (e.g., popular Islam in North Africa, permeated by the cult of the saints, the influence of Mazdaism in Iran, traces of which are found in the Shiism of present-day Iran).

Then came decadence.

III. *Islam confronts the modern world.*

Islam was drawn into the 19th century of decadence by its brutal encounter with the West; this could be considered the renaissance which culminated in modern Islam.

Islam, which was conscious of being the order willed by God, realized it was behind the West. From this arose the crisis which is in full swing before our eyes, a crisis that can be attributed to three attitudes toward the modern world:

a) If the West has dominated us, it is because we were not faithful to Islam. We must therefore return to the sources (cf. Malek Bennabi, *Vocation of Islam*).

b) The West is wrong. Let us remain the way we are; in the end, we will be right (Koranic Universities).

c) The West has surpassed us. The cause of this backwardness is Islam. It must therefore be rejected. There follows a temptation to Marxism, especially in the student world which is struck by the example of Russia and China.

It is with this Islam in crisis that we Christians must come into contact. The contact seems easy. There are words in common, and the vocabulary does not alienate us: monotheism, prophet, retribution, hell, paradise, creation, almsgiving. These notions are similar—they are of Christian origin. Islam developed in the 7th century A.D. in Christian countries. There are historical contacts between Mohammed and Judeo-Christian thought, attested to by the Koran itself.

But this apparently easy contact is not immediate, because these notions which seem to be in common were at the outset emptied of their Christian substance. In Islam everything holds together. The meaning of words and of theology can only be attained through historical, political, social reality. In other words, words which we have in common do not have the same meaning for us and for the Moslems.

Islam extolls a unique God, we proclaim the Trinity. For the Moslems, Abraham is the prophet of monotheism; for us, he is the prophet of the Covenant.

From the outset, the notions borrowed from Christianity were considered in a different light, and this difference sharpened with time. Islam today is much further removed from Christianity than it was at its origin. Apologists such as St. John Damascene considered Islam as a Christian heresy, not as a different religion. Today it would be difficult to make a similar judgment.

In our contacts with Islam, we have to know who we are and just what the other party is. We have to know what we are saying when we speak. We must realize that the contact is not immediate and that we must accept the other side for what it is. Then, there must be a movement of return to the sources. The Koran is closer to Christianity than modern-day Islam. We must try to re-discover the Christian value in Moslem realities, perhaps demonstrate that a different development from that accomplished by Islam is possible. We must carry on concrete activity with the Moslems in order to be mutually enriched by understanding and charity.

4. FRANCOIS HOUANG | BUDDHISM

People often think that Buddhism is a universal religion which remains identical in all Buddhist countries. But as a matter of fact, there are different tendencies: the "Small Vehicle" is widespread in Ceylon, Cambodia, Laos, Thailand and Burma; the "Grand Vehicle," in China, Japan, Korea and North Vietnam. To these two categories must be added Tibetan Lamaism, a mixture of the Buddhism of the "Grand Vehicle" and local religious practices.

The adherents of the "Grand Vehicle" (*mahâyâna*) assign the name "Small Vehicle" or "lesser vehicle" (*hînayâna*) to the rule of life and the method of salvation of the ancient monastic schools. These schools claim a dogmatic tradition for themselves going back to Buddha himself.

The "Grand Vehicle" does not contest this claim, but boasts of "conveying" farther and more conveniently a greater number of creatures, whence its name. It acknowledges that it is a new Buddhism, a new doctrine of salvation, based on a more profound interpretation of the ancient texts and a more faithful understanding of the spirit of Buddha.

In order to have a good understanding of Buddhism, and to form a complete idea of it, it would therefore be necessary ot consider it in its multiple tendencies.

There is a great deal of talk today about the renewal of Buddhism (cf. the celebration of the 2,500th anniversary of the death of the Buddha in 1956, in Burma and India). But it does not seem likely that there will be a reunion of these two "vehicles" of Buddhism in the immediate future, since the difference between the Sino-Japanese Buddhism and that of Ceylon is greater than that between Protestantism and Catholicism.

The Life of Buddha

Among the founders of religions, the Buddha was the only one not to claim to be an inspired messenger. He says: "You have to do your own work, the perfect ones only show you the way." As opposed to Christianity, Buddhism does not rely on any *supernatural revelation*.

a) *Chronology*

His chronology is submerged in the legendary traditions which do not even permit us to be sure of the dates. According to the traditions of Ceylon, the historical Buddha is supposed to have lived from 623 to 543 B.C., but, according to the calculations of modern science, his dates are figured to be from 560 to 480 B.C.

b) *Biography*

The documents we have on the life of Buddha are several centuries later than the historical events. They indicate that the community which transmitted them had admitted a great number of mythological and miraculous elements. By eliminating these excrescences, it is possible to reconstitute a more plausible "life of Buddha."

—His given name was Siddhârtha and his family name was Gautama.
—He was born not into the Brahman caste but of a

princely family—the clan of Sakyas, established at Kapilavastu, mid-way between the middle course of the Ganges and the Himalayas, in a region now part of Nepal and therefore far removed from the centers of Brahmanism.

—At the age of 29, he left the family circle to seek a path of deliverance, but neither the teachings of the *Upanishads* nor ascetic mortifications satisfied him.

—At the age of 35, he ended up accomplishing his own awakening (*bodhi*) and became an awakened one (*buddha*). He preached his first sermon at Benares.

—This preaching won him 5 disciples, the nucleus of the first community (*sangha*).

—After this, for 45 years, he led the life of a wanderer, teaching his doctrine.

—He died at the age of 80. To his community, already considerable, he left only his Law.

The Doctrine

The historical Buddha inherited from Hinduism:

a) belief in the inevitable and mechanical retribution for actions (*karman*) whether good or bad.
b) belief in transmigration (*samsara*) through a cycle of successive births and deaths.

But the Buddha revolted against the philosophic tendencies of the Hinduism of his time (the *Upanishads*).

For the *Upanishads* (the philosophic treatises), salvation lies in the identification of the human self (*atman*) with the universal principle (*Brahman*), of the empirical soul with the absolute soul.

For Buddha, there is no being in the self. Personality is an illusion, it is only a transitory assemblage of aggregates; everything is non-permanent, everything is a composite and therefore subject to decomposition. Buddha was looking not for an identification of the finite self with the absolute self on the ontological level, but in a practical way, a *therapy*, a discipline of salvation.

The doctrine of the *four holy truths* as contained in the sermon preached by the Buddha at Benares constitutes the basis of his teaching.

These four holy truths (or four noble truths) are:

1) the ascertainment of suffering (*dukkha*); this is the *diagnosis*;
2) the origin of the suffering; this is the *etiology*;
3) the cessation of the suffering; this is the *healing*;
4) the path which leads to the cessation of suffering; this is the *therapy* itself.

Diagnosis: In what does the evil consist?

In suffering, which is a universal fact. To exist is to suffer; this comes very close to the Christian position. However, let us note that the concept of suffering (*dukkha*) includes not only physical pain and all forms of suffering encountered in life (old age, death, etc.) but also everything connected with painful situations (for instance, being separated from loved ones, not obtaining what one desires, sadness, sorrow, distress, anguish, etc.).

What complicates the Buddhist doctrine of suffering even more, is belief in transmigration. Our present life will be continued in a new life and new sorrows. This round of existences is governed by the law of causality. Everything that exists is born in dependence on a cause and is destroyed giving birth to something else, the same current of energy passing through this endless chain of causes and effects. This is the causal current, thanks to which each of our actions inevitably draws its consequences with it into another existence.

Etiology: What is the origin or cause of suffering?

Desire, greed, "thirst"—thirst for sensual pleasures, thirst for existence, for continuity, and even desire for annihilation. This avidity, this thirst, which is based on a false idea of a "self" is a terrible force which carries all existence along with it. At the moment of death, unfulfilled desires will bring on a new re-birth and the painful cycle will be continued.

Healing: How to heal the ailment, that is, to cease suffering?

To have no more desire, to cease having the "thirst" for existence. In order to destroy suffering absolutely, it is necessary to eliminate its root which is this desire, this thirst. Since our actions follow us for both good and evil, creating an ascending and a descending ladder for another existence in the process of transmigration, we must find an "escape" from this sealed chamber. It is even useless to believe in the gods, because, being finite, they too cannot escape from the eternal law of the re-birth of desire. There is but one remedy left: *nirvana* (extinction of desire or thirst). This is the state to which one arrives when desire has been extinguished. Is it a conscious state or an unconscious state? The Buddha never gave a precise reply to this.

Therapy: What path should be followed?

This is a "middle way," avoiding two extremes: the pursuit of happiness in the attachment to sensual pleasures, and the practice of ascetic mortifications. This "middle way" gives knowledge and leads to the awakening, to *nirvana.* It is an "eight-branch road" because it is composed of eight factors.

Two *intellectual* factors: correct understanding
correct thinking

Three *moral* factors: correct speech
correct action
correct way of living.

Three factors deriving from *mental discipline*:
correct effort
correct attention
correct concentration.

Thus, in Buddhism, awakening must be preceded by active morality and intellectual vision. The practice of the precepts—not to kill, not to lie, not to have illicit sexual relations, not to consume alcoholic beverages, not to steal—as well as the exercise of the positive virtues—good will for all beings, forgiveness of injuries, etc.—are just as important for the awakening (*bodhi*) as the knowledge of the four holy truths. Buddha does not reject *yoga*, but attaches only a secondary importance to it.

This is the doctrine the Buddha is supposed to have taught himself. He never wrote anything, the entire tradition is oral. Inscriptions of King Asoka have been found which mention Buddhist texts, but without any precise references. It is likely that the scriptural Rule[1] available to us was established after Asoka (middle of the 3rd century B.C.).

---

[1] The Buddhist Rule of the "Small Vehicle" includes the *texts* (*sutras*), that is, the discourses and conversations of the Buddha with his disciples, the *discipline* (*vinaya*) or monastic rule, and the *exegesis* (*abhidharma*). This is what we call the *Three Baskets* (*tripitaka*).

Buddhism in India

During the first century of our era, Buddhism broke up into two branches: the Small Vehicle and the Grand Vehicle.

The Schools of the Small Vehicle

According to tradition, the two oldest schools are the Ancients (*sthavira*), the designation for the elders of a community, and the Majoritarians (*mahâsanghika*), "those of the Great Community." The former were conservative and strict in matters of monastic discipline, and the latter more liberal, inclined to make the doctrine of the Buddha accessible to the laity. The former had as their religious ideal the *arhat*, the holy for its own sake, and the latter tended to make the Buddha a supra-terrestrial being (*lokottara*).

In the monasteries, there was a great deal of discussion at the time in an attempt to resolve the conflict between the causality of acts whose effects are perpetuated in time for the duration of transmigration, and the non-existence of a permanent "self" conceived as moral agent. From this came

---

This rule, written in the Pali language, belonged especially to the school of the Ancients and was only one of the rules of the schools of the "Small Vehicle." As to the "Grand Vehicle," there are other rules. The Chinese rule, for instance, is an indescribable mixture of *sutras*, *vinaya*, and all the treatises and writings either translated from the Sanskrit or written directly in Chinese. Studying Chinese Buddhism through the texts would therefore be a tremendous task. It would be as if one were to assemble loosely in the Catholic canon the Scriptures, the works of exegesis and biblical commentaries, dogmatic definitions, monastic constitutions, canon law, the Fathers of the Church, spiritual writings, the controversies of theologians, etc. An example of the complexity of the texts: a well-known treatise in China, "The Awakening of the Faith of the Grand Vehicle," had always been attributed to the Indian Buddhist philosopher Asvaghosha, but it now is found that it was purely a Chinese creation of the sixth century A.D.

the formation of two other, later, schools: the *Sarvastivadins* (everything exists) and the *Sautrantika* (partisans of the sutras).

The first of these schools is pan-realist and atomistic. There is no "self," but only a transitory assemblage of aggregates. Transmigration is explained by the existence of three temporal modalities: past, present and future. Because of this, acts may have continuity in time.

The second school admits only the existence of the present. To explain retribution for actions, it postulates that the present is heavy with the past and pregnant with the future. Our actions contain germs which will be apt to bear fruit in another existence.

The Grand Vehicle

The Majoritarians are generally thought of as the forerunners of the Grand Vehicle. The Mahâyâna definitively appeared in the first century of our era. It probably had been pushed by the lay movement.

Points of difference from the Hinayana:

1) *Religious ideal*

Where in the Small Vehicle, which is essentially monastic, the religious ideal is the *arhat*, the holy for its own sake (mastery of the passions, of desire, the search for nirvana), in the Grand Vehicle we arrive at the universality of Salvation. The Buddha renounced entering nirvana in order to save all the others. The "Boddhisattvas," aspirant-Buddhas or candidates for Boddheity through the practice of the active and heroic virtues of charity and sacrifice, seek to lead all beings to salvation. The *Boddhisattva* thus becomes the religious ideal of all Buddhists, monks or laymen.

2) *Deification of the Buddha*

In the Small Vehicle, the historical Buddha is in no way divine; he is a doctor of the law, he who has shown us the way of salvation. But in the Grand Vehicle, the historical Buddha no longer has any importance; what matters is a supra-terrestrial, deified, Buddha. There is a multiplication of Buddhas and Boddhisattvas. The Amitabha, infinite life and infinite light, begins to assume a great importance in the popular cult in the countries of the Far East. Buddhism thus becomes a religion of grace and of the reversibility of merits, with the Boddhisattvas in effect playing the role of intercessors.

The existence of Paradises where the Buddhas are enthroned—such as the Paradise of the West, land of beatitude —is even postulated.

3) *Metaphysical concept*

While the schools of the Small Vehicle reduced everything to elements and proclaimed a kind of realism, the Grand Vehicle implies an idealistic philosophy. The compassion and the wisdom of the Buddha are simply the compassion and wisdom of the Absolute Himself. (Here we re-discover the absolute of the Upanishads.) The Grand Vehicle identifies the Absolute with *Dharmakaya*, that is, the *Body of the Law* of Buddha, which is superior to his body of flesh.

The Two Great Schools of the Grand Vehicle

1) *Mâdhyamika*

(School of the middle) or *sunyavâda* (school of the void): the Absolute is outside our conceptual, discursive thinking, which is full of contradictions; one can only reach the Absolute, this "Void," by means of a supra-relational intuition wherein duality is neutralized (cf. the absolute idealism of the Englishman Bradley).

2) *Vijnânavâda*

(School of the theory of knowledge): nothing exists outside our knowledge, our thought, our mind. This is a subjective idealism. The external world is but the illusory product of our minds.

Buddhism disappeared from India at the end of the 10th century A.D.

Causes:
1) The hostility of the Brahmans who clung to the caste system.
2) The absorption of the "Grand Vehicle" Buddhism by Hinduism.
3) The invasion of Islam.

The Buddhism of the "Small Vehicle" spread particularly into the countries of South Asia, and the Grand Vehicle into the countries of the Far East.

For several centuries now, Buddhism had lost its religious vitality. But, beginning in the last century under the influence of the West and in reaction to it, attempts at a renewal have been made.

5. MAURICE QUEGUINER, P.F.M. | HINDUISM

It is reckless to plan to sum up Hinduism in one essay. This subject is a vast, nearly unfathomable ocean. We shall attempt to distinguish three parts of it here:

1. Key notions of Hinduism; 2. Authority and Scriptures; 3. Modern reformers of Hinduism.

I. *Key Notions of Hinduism*

Hinduism is a *religion of salvation.* But salvation from what? Essentially from the *samsara*: the cycle of re-births, of re-incarnations.

Initially, the Hindus did not seek to justify this belief in transmigration, one of the most widespread in the human soul. Later on, they explained it by the law of *karma* or the fructification of actions. Every act bears two kinds of fruit: a fruit of the emotional order, happiness, unhappiness; and the fruit of a further action. At death, every man has a balance sheet of good or of evil; in order that he may be freed, his account must balance out at zero. It is not enough for the good to outweigh the evil, that is, that there be no further sanctions to be applied for previous actions, but there must be no further need for action deriving from a former action. It is certain that inequality strikes men from birth. On the other hand, this inequality involves a whole range of sufferings, of injustices shocking to our sense of equity. To explain all this, Hinduism invented this law of *karma*.

There are three kinds of *karmas*:

—The *parabhdha karma* one brings with him at birth: heredity, sex. For the Hindu, being a woman is a handicap, for the woman is considered as an impure being—the female sex is a consequence of evil actions in a former existence.

This capital granted at birth can be transformed by the efforts of our free will. Temperament is thus changed into character.

—From this, we have the *sankita karma*, acquired in this existence through the good or bad use of the birth karma.

—Finally, the karma-in-process which one may or may not acquire according to one's present dispositions, the *agami karma*.

In other words, the karma of birth is the arrow already shot, the second karma is the arrow on the taut bowstring, and the third is the arrow in the quiver.

Let us consider the dynamic aspect of the law of the karma, that is to say, *the paths of salvation*.

For all Hindus, the non-delivered soul is united with the rough body through the intermediary of a fine body, the principle of individuation which differentiates men one from the other. While the rough body only appears at birth and disappears at death, the fine body accompanies the soul from all eternity, and will not leave it until deliverance.

Proof of this is the fact that existence is not happy, that sorrow outweighs happiness. This is why it is well to leave this flesh (the *samsara*) by obtaining salvation (*mukti*). Liberation from transmigration is conceived in different ways according to the various philosophical schools of India. There are three paths along which it may be reached:

The path of action, *karma yoga*; the path of loving adoration, *bhakti yoga*; the path of knowledge, of the contemplative gnosis, *jnana yoga*.

A. *Path of action: karma yoga*

What action leads to deliverance? Every action creates a balance sheet of pleasure and sorrow, and then a further need for action. However, there are two exceptions: disinterested action which produces no fruit, no further karma, and actions indifferent from the moral point of view (drinking, eating, going, coming).

The karma yoga consists in the integral practice of the *dharma*. The dharma is the power, the order which sustains the universe, the cosmic order, the rhythm of the seasons. This is the law that must be observed, the rule of personal behavior, in short, this is religion. Religion is a wisdom, a technique. In Hinduism, philosophy is not distinguished from religion.

The universal dharma becomes concrete on the threefold level of social, family and personal life; whence the three aspects of the dharma: 1) *varnadharma*, the law of the castes; 2) *ashramadharma*, the law of the states of life; 3) *svadharma*, the law of personal behavior.

1) *Varnadharma* (from "varna": color): this theory of castes is a consequence of the invasions of India by peoples of different races and different colors (e.g. the Aryans were less dark-skinned than the Dravidians or the Shudras, the first inhabitants of India).

The caste law seeks to preserve the purity of the race. Therefore, anything that can soil one must be avoided, and especially two things: *conviviality* or eating together—one does not take food with a man of a caste inferior to one's own, or partake of dishes prepared by him. (If there are superior castes and inferior castes, this is because there are in society inferior occupations which require that one approach impure things: butcher, barber, pedicurist, hairdresser, physician, nurse); and *connubiality*—one marries within one's caste. If one goes against the laws of caste, one falls among the "out-castes."

The present division of castes is explained by mythology: the *Brahmans* are supposed to come from the head of Brahma; they are the depositories of knowledge, they are the light and the guides of the people. Then the brave ones, *khshatriyas*, come from his shoulders: these are the warriors. The *vaîshyas*, men of business and finance, come from the belly. Finally, the *shudras*, men devoted to physical labors, come from his feet.

Outside of these four classic castes, themselves divided into three or four thousand sub-castes, there are the *untouchables* or out-castes, whose touch, whose shadow even, contaminates. The present Government of India, in the Constitution of 1950, condemned untouchability and provided penalties for those who forbid the pariahs to wear certain items of clothing, access to certain streets, etc.

Strangers or *netchas* are in an even more deplorable religious state. Their previous existence has prevented them from acceding to the dharma. Gandhi saw to it that this untouchability was condemned by the Constitution. It will be far more difficult to eliminate it from the mores.

2) *Ashramadharma*: the law of the states of life. Investiture with the sacred cord, initiation to the duties of the caste, introduce the Hindu to adulthood (age of reason). Beginning with this second birth, he passes successively through several states of life:

a) State of life of the student who practices chastity and penance during his entire time of studies.
b) Phase of the head of the family: every man will marry, found a family, for a man must have a son to light his funeral pyre, otherwise the father's soul will wander for years before finding a favorable re-incarnation.
c) After having pursued the worldly ends of life (acquisition of wealth, pleasure . . .), after having raised his children, a man retires from the world, lives in seclusion with his wife, abandoning himself to contemplation, detaching himself from the world even to the point of separating from his wife to live as a hermit in the forest: he becomes a "renouncer", *sanyasi*. At this stage he is dead to the world. In orthodox India, he is dead to society, he can no longer return into civic life—though modern laws have permitted it for several years now.

3) *Svadharma*: the law of personal behavior. Every man has a particular vision of the world, of himself, of God. He has a power of discernment which brings it about that after a certain period of existence his notions are different from those of childhood, from those of his neighbor, etc. At a given time in his life, a man placed in certain circumstances sees his duty in a certain definite way. His conscience is quite specially informed to take such and such a decision. This element corresponds somewhat to today's situation morality: one must act according to one's lights and one's power in the particular conditions in which one is placed.

After having set forth the laws of salvation, Hinduism defines its techniques. These are devotion, worship, sacrifice offered to God, prayer, etc. This cult has two aspects:

—Recited prayer (*mantra*) has a particular significance in Hinduism, because the voice, the breath, are an incarnation of God. Hinduism's exercises of piety are similar to certain practices of oriental Christianity which have the name of God being repeated, identifying it with God. The repetition of the "mantra" is their "rosary" (with 108 beads because there are 108 Upanishads): "God is my refuge . . . God is my refuge . . ."

—The *mudras*, Indian dances in which the gestures of the hands and face express religious convictions.

To be instructed in all these methods, one must have recourse to the *guru*, the spiritual teacher, the director of conscience, far more vital than in Christianity. The guru is one who has realized the truth. The truth, for the Hindus, is something pragmatic. It is the spiritual experience which counts more than anything else. The guru has experienced the divine, illumination. The disciple will be subjected to many tests, the guru will instruct him by communicating to him methods of prayer, transmitting to him the illumination of the faith, by a contact, a word, etc. Faith in the guru is something very important.

Every day the pious orthodox Hindu resorts to prayer, and his entire day is dominated by prayer (meals, action, etc.) The sense of the divine presence and the concern for purity intervene in his entire life.

B. *The loving devotion: bhakti yoga*

This aspect of the Hindu religion greatly resembles the illuminative way of Christian contemplation. At first glance, the way of action may seem the clearest and most sure. Experience has shown, however, that pure disinterestedness, the essential condition for action, is a human ideal impossible to achieve. Therefore, men have sought to find short-cuts to attain liberation more quickly.

Salvation is a gift of God. It cannot be merited . . . He gives it. This is preached in the Bhagavad Gita, the hymn of the Lord. The god Krishna says: "Concentrate on me; adore me and you will come to me; leave all your obligations behind and take me as your refuge." One must attain *bhakti*, that is, total union: ". . . A leaf, a flower, a fruit or some water . . . whatsoever you do, do it as an offering to me." There are Christian overtones here; salvation can come only from God—"He who loves God has neither desire nor sorrow."

This love will be dominant throughout the life of the bhakta (he who practices bhakti). But it takes two to have love. What then is God in Hinduism? Here we find the pantheistic concept of Shankara. In terms of appearances, the striking thing about India is the large number of officially recognized gods (33 million gods, trees, statues, rivers, stones . . .) But in fact, there is something else over and above that. To practice bhakti, God is conceived as a person. For the orthodox Hindu philosopher, these days, God is someone supra-personal, infinite, transcendent, incomprehensible. He can be spoken of only by negation. He is defined as "the one without a second."

Hinduism has tried to personalize God by giving Him three main functions—it has considered Him under three names: Brahma (creator), Vishnu (preserver), Shiva (transformer, who ensures the cyclical movement of the universe). But, we should not speak of a Hindu triad, but rather of a Hindu pleiad, since the goddesses and the divine energies are personalized, too. Indeed, the divinity is neither male nor female, neither father nor mother, but both of them at once. The bhakta selects one of these aspects of God and adores it.

The incarnations of God are varied (Krishna, Vishnu). They are avatars, descents: theophanies. When anarchy triumphs in the world and the law is no longer respected, Krishna becomes incarnate. He comes to reject the wicked. Though there are in the human body, in the primary matter, three elements—an obscure element of inertia (*tamas*), an element of dynamism (*rajas*), and an element of purity (*sattva*)—the gods only take this last element, purity. They do not become men, in contrast to the Christian Incarnation in which God, while remaining God, becomes truly man. Here the god only assumes the appearance of a man—it is a theophany.

The Hindu renders to the god a *worship*, *puja*, in several parts. Its goal is to cause the divinity to descend into a statuette. He prepares the statue, spreads it with melted sugar (very precious material), perfumes, offers it garlands of flowers, incense, and then takes leave of the divinity. A very realistic worship which scans the entire day of the divinity, from dawn to dusk. (Cf. ceremonies at the great temples.)

The bhakta surrenders himself wholly to God who is his refuge; this is total abandonment to the divinity. There has been some discussion among the philosophers to decide whether man has to cooperate in his own salvation by personal effort, whether he has to correspond to grace in a positive way. Some say yes, others no. There are therefore different concepts of "grace" in this practice of the bhakti, just as there are in Hinduism multiple aspects of the divinity and of devotion, and one does not exclude the reality of the others.

C. *Way of the gnosis: jnana yoga*

This is the summit of philosophical speculation. The *jnana* is at once knowledge and experience of God. For the *jnanin*, the soul is already liberated, but it does not know it. The manifold manifestations of the contingent blind it. It is necessary to tear away this veil which universal illusion weaves around the spirit. The greatest error is to believe in an individual self which is distinct and different from the universal self or Atman. All sensible experience nourishes this error; personality is merely a welter of appearances around an illusory center of reference and possession. Ignorance is responsible for this fantastic deception. It is knowledge, therefore, that will do justice to reality—not a simple notional knowledge, but living knowledge tested by the truth and expressed in the words: "You are *that*"—that signifying the Atman, the Absolute, the unutterable Universal.

Nevertheless, the abyss between the daily experience of the manifold contingent and the extremely rare experience of identification with the One, acquired in ecstasy, is so great that it is practically impossible to cross it directly. Also, the individual being, prisoner of the samsara from time immemorial, must still migrate for the purpose of complete purification through numerous existences before attaining that maturity which is the threshold of salvation.

II. *Authorities and Scriptures*

Hinduism has no founder, no constitutional church, no doctrinal magisterium. It does not rest on a revelation, nor on individual reason. Its ultimate authority is the experience of a host of beliefs, or ancient mystiques, an experience which everyone must make his own by bending to a certain discipline. The Hindu concept of religious truth is essentially pragmatic and subjective. It does, however, rely upon writings relating to the believers of a former age and the speculations of their disciples.

There are two sorts of scriptures:

—The *sruti*, "that which is understood," contains the revelations of the ancient sages regarding the nature of God, of man, of the world. The books containing these revelations transmitted to their disciples are divided into three categories: the Vedas, the Brahmins, the Upanishads.

1) The "*samhitas*" or *Vedas*, properly so-called, written between 1500 and 800 B.C., are the most ancient collections of hymns or formulas. In them, God is called the Infinite, but certain types of animisms are also found there: all the forces of nature are divinized (wind, storm). Each in turn is personalized and considered as the supreme force. Man has personal contacts with these gods. Sin is already a personal fault and not a physico-moral sickness.

2) In the *Brahmins*, written between 800 and 700, the perspective is different. The priest has become an important personage. The great force of the world is sacrifice. Whoever is master of sacrifice is the master of the world. Sacrifice sets in motion the secret force to which the gods and the universe give their obedience. "The sun would not rise if the priest did not offer sacrifice to make it rise."

Here sacrifice is magic. All it takes is to perform certain actions with precision and the power of the universe is at the disposal of the priest. And it is through sacrifice that Prajapati, the Lord of creatures, produced the world. God is therefore no longer at the center of the religion; sacrifice is. Thus, religion becomes ritualism.

3) Dating from 700 to 650 B.C., the *Upanishads* are a reaction against this formalism and materialism of sacrifices. In the eyes of the Hindu, they are the highest, the most perfect, expression of the divine revelation. They include speculations on the nature of God and the world.

—The *smriti*, "that which is remembered," includes the whole of the secondary scriptures commenting on and developing the teachings of the sruti.

The smriti is divided into five classes of works:

1) the smriti proper, codes and collections of laws governing Hindu society.

2) the "itihasas", epic stories and poems. Eighty per cent of the people of India are illiterate, but they are as a rule very cultured, because the family transmits tradition. Two great poems, the *Ramayana* and the *Mahabharata*, are worthy of special note. In the second poem, the *Bhagavad-Gita* or hymn of the Lord, is a panegyric of disinterested action, of power in the fulfillment of duty. The god Krishna constructs in it a whole philosophy of life, of action, of bhakti, of yoga.

3) the *puranas*, or collection of geneologies, legends and narratives concerning the avatars of the gods.

4) the *agamas* or books of the sects.

5) the *darsanas* or philosophical systems of India.

The classical *Yoga* is a particular way which aims at emancipation through the immobility of the spirit in mystical absorption. Derived from the root *Yuj*, to yoke together, to unite, the word signifies tension or union. If one thinks of yoga as systematic training of the mind, then it can be defined as tension; if it is considered insofar as it is a mystical path toward God, it will naturally be defined as union.

For Patanjali, in the second century B.C., the goal of

yoga seemed to be the complete transparency of the mind to itself through the purification of the states of consciousness. As a system, it is based on the dualistic concept of the *sankhya*: man is composed of mind and matter. It is a question of gaining perfect possession of the self by asceticism, so that the mind, instead of being imprisoned beneath the physical and psychic layers which constitute our ordinary lives, governs and is in a position to judge the truth of things, and above all, to comprehend itself, without intermediary, in its own being.

This yoga, referred to as royal, involves a moral, intellectual and psycho-physical discipline whose elements can be divided into five groups of indirect means of concentration, and three degrees of contemplation.

The indirect means, or practical Yoga

The first group includes abstention from violence, lying, theft, impurity, of the greed which leads to the accepting of gifts (*yama*). Then comes the practical application of the five rules for exterior and interior purification: bodily and spiritual purity, sobriety, asceticism, study and abandonment to God. Thirdly, we have certain postures (*asana*) favorable to bodily balance and to meditation. Then, the regulation of breathing (*pranayama*) which favors interior tranquillity. Fifth and last, there is the withdrawal of the sense organs far from objects (*pratyahana*).

Degrees of contemplation

The first (*dhârana*) is the fixing of attention on one certain object: the navel, the end of the nose or of the tongue. The second is the intensification of attention to the point that all foreign representations are excluded and the object chosen for concentration fills the whole mind. The third, or *samâdhi*, is the identification of the thought with the form of the object, though in the inferior phase (*samprajnata*), there remains the awareness of the presence of an object, while in the higher phase (*asamprajnata*), even the representation of an object is suspended. Here the subject himself is the object of concentration and if the absorption in self lasts long, the *karma* is annihilated and the spirit is delivered.

Having arrived at perfection, the yogi can put into operation the extraordinary powers which, according to him, are not miraculous, but which exceed the capacity of ordinary men: he can make himself, at will, microscopic, invisible or gigantic; he can read into the mind of others, know the past, the present, the future; act at a distance, etc.

Patanjali's classical Yoga underwent a very diversified evolution. The sects were to appropriate his method for themselves; thus, the royal Yoga little by little yielded the primacy to three other yogas: the Mantra-yoga, which seeks liberation through the repetition of sacred syllables (particularly *Om*) in which mystical powers dwell; the Hatha-yoga, which, through violent efforts (*hatha*), such as the adoption of painful positions, certain breathing exercises and certain sexual practices, seeks to purify the channels of the body and to create the conditions favorable for meditation; finally, the Laya-yoga, founded on a particular anatomy of man. The body is supposed to include an extraordinary number of canals or *nadis*, traversing man through and through; but the most important one is the *sushumma*, a large vein located in the vertebral column where it connects the head with the trunk, and shelters man's energy nodes: six circles (*chakra*), or lotus-flowers (*padma*), dominated by a seventh at the peak of the cranium. On the bottom circle, in the form of a coiled serpent, is the *kunda-*

lini, the goddess Shakti or the force of nature, Prakriti. Above the sixth circle dwells her husband Shiva, the Purusha, or spirit. The practice of yoga consists in awakening the *kundalini*, through a special process, so that she can ascend through the circles to the dwelling-place of Shiva in order to be united to him. After having enjoyed this union, the *kundalini* returns to her own place, until, having acquired the habit, she remains with her husband forever, one with him, absorbed (*laya*) in him. The shaktas consider this yoga as the highest, but since the ecstasy involved is aware (of its object), it is supposed to be inferior to the Raja-yoga which leads to non-conscient mystical absorption, the only one which guarantees complete and definitive liberation from all bonds.

The sect which espouses these procedures, Tantrism, is in the minority in India; however, Westerners have exploited its theories for commercial ends.

From what has been said here, it is easy to determine one of the essential differences between Hinduism and Catholicism. For us, as Christians, renunciation is not automatism or even at best, essence of mystical experience, but humble and penitent preparation for the grace merited by Christ, the initiative for which rests always with God.

III. *Modern reforms and reformers*

It would take a whole study to speak of the present vitality of Hinduism. In the 19th century, the preaching of Protestant and Catholic missionaries aroused among the elite of the country feelings of shame about idolatry and polytheism. The re-awakening of Hinduism and several reform movements were the result.

1) The *Brahmo-Samaj* is a monotheistic sect founded by Raja Ram Mohan Roy, the father of modern India. A passionately religious spirit profoundly influenced by Islam and by Christianity, he waged a determined struggle against polytheism and social abuses. In 1820, he published a book on *The Precepts of Jesus, a Guide to Happiness*, and in 1828, he founded the Brahmo-Samaj or Church of Brahma, "open to men of all categories and conditions, for the worship and adoration of the eternal, impenetrable and immortal Being who is the Creator and Preserver of the universe."

The insistence on the existence of one God, on providence, prayer, repentance, testifies to the Christian influence. And modern Hinduism cannot be understood without this syncretist Brahmo-Samaj movement.

2) The *Arya-Samaj*, founded by Swami Dayanand Saraswati, preaches a return to the Vedas. For its promoter, orthodox Hinduism was monotheism without idolatry, without caste, and without sacrifice. However, he did not find merely spiritual sustenance in the Vedas. According to him, all profane knowledge as well emanated from these books: locomotives, airplanes, etc., everything was hidden therein, one had only to be able to read them. On the other hand, everything that was foreign had to disappear. Whence an ardent proselytism aimed at extirpating Christianity and Islam. Finally, Dayanand Saraswati, a man of action, concerned himself with numerous social questions in India, all of which contributed to the important development of the Arya-Samaj.

3) *Ramakrishna*. Whereas the preceding sects were oriented toward an ever-narrower exclusiveness, and proclaimed the superiority of the Hindu religion over all other

forms of faith, a Bengali ascetic and mystic named Ramakrishna Paramahamsa taught, on the contrary, that all religions were equally good, equally true.

His most famous disciple, Swami Vivekananda, imparted a systematic aspect to his master's teachings and spread them, especially in America. The non-dualism of Shankara (idealist and pantheistic monism of the One without second, the Absolute), became, with him, the official doctrine of the movement, which explains its aggressive attitude against Christianity and Islam.

In 1893, in Chicago, Vivekananda founded the *Ramakrishna Mission*, devoted to proselytism, which is contrary to the slogan of the equality of religions. This is one of the most extraordinary religious accomplishments of modern India. It has thrown itself into the work of educating youth and of charity toward the poor.

4) *Shri Aurobindo Ghose*. Speculative Hinduism was represented in the modern era by Shri Aurobindo Ghose (1872-1950), the founder of the famous Ashram of Pondicherry, where several hundreds of his followers have continued, since his death, leading a vedic life under the direction of the Mother, the wife and principal disciple of Aurobindo who re-thought Hinduism in a Bergsonian perspective.

5) *Gandhi* would need a book by himself. He stamped Hinduism by his struggle against untouchability, by his cult of the truth, his love of non-violence; he was not a religious reformer as such, but he was inspired by religious principles in his political and social activities. By putting religion at the service of politics, he made it slightly ambiguous. He was truly the symbol of committed Hinduism, but of a Hinduism whose dynamism came primarily from the Gospels.

Indian religious life, rich and manifold in its expressions, includes numerous points of contact with Christianity. Life of faith, life of adoration and prayer, life of penance, liturgical life, these undoubtedly form stepping-stones to a real Revelation of God in the Hindu soul profoundly receptive to the sense of the sacred.

Still, we cannot ignore the fact that these points of similarity become in practice stumbling-blocks or at least invitations to indifferentism, syncretism or confusion. The syncretist spirit of tolerance is paradoxically and logically joined to official intolerance toward the Christian missionary apostolate directly confronting this supposedly "absorbent" Hinduism. On the doctrinal level, the differences are deep: the only God disappears into pantheism, ignorance of the notion of creation positively excludes any idea of transcendence; rites and sacrifices do not go beyond the signs; and the "incarnations," shivaite or otherwise, do not lead to the unique Incarnation.

6. R. P. DUNOYER, P.F.M.

THE RELIGIONS OF JAPAN

In Japan there are two great religions, Shintoism and Buddhism. First, Shintoism, a specifically national religion which, however, over the centuries was subject to different influences such as Confucianism from China and Buddhism. Buddhism, imported from India through China, is divided into innumerable sects in which, at least in some cases, the fundamental ideas of Buddhism are either missing or hardly noticeable.

To these two great religious currents, one would have to add many other sects, many other churches, which abound in the Japan of 1960: *seichono ie*, *Tenrikyo*, *Kongokyo*, "the religion of the dance," etc. There are indeed so many sects that this study of the religions of Japan can be only a rapid overflight of several main religious currents and should rather be entitled—with apologies to Fr. Brémond—"History of Religious Feeling in Japan."

I. *Shintoism: the "way of the gods."*

What is Shintoism? The original religion of the Japanese people, a very primitive cult of nature in the form of fetishistic animism. The fundamental belief of Shintoism is an idea which can be expressed as follows: everything which, in the world of nature, possesses power, beauty, or charm, everything which is gracious and sweet, participates in divinity, shelters it and reveals it: the sea, the sun, the moon, the cliff, the flower along the riverbank, the tree. With this belief as a starting point, it is quite certain that the religious sentiment in Japan will consist in a poetic intimacy with nature and the gods, in a feeling of gratitude, of thankfulness and of joy over so much beauty. This is the second great idea of Shintoism: unlike other peoples, the Japanese experience no feeling of fear in the presence of nature. Among them, there is no conflict between nature and man considered as a creature who has his place in creation and is linked to it by an ontological bond. From this stems the feeling of incurable optimism which catches the attention of every foreigner who comes in contact with a Japanese. Nature is good and faithful. There is great joy in living in communion with the universe and the gods.

Each year, the publishing houses of Paris organize a competition among students of French in foreign countries. First prize consists of a grant for a year of study in Paris. The winner for the year 1959 was a Japanese girl student from Tokyo. When she was interviewed by newsmen on her impressions at the end of her stay in Paris, she confessed very candidly that while she certainly loved the ancient stones of Paris, she really found Westerners far too restless and preferred the serenity of the Far East. Indeed, metaphysical unrest, the search for the truth, does not torture the Japanese soul.

In concrete terms, what is the content of the Shintoist faith? Belief in an infinity of tutelary gods derived in the beginning from a solar myth. Here is a resumé of this theogony as found in a Japanese classic, the *Nihonshoki*, written around 710 A.D., the age of Nara. It is a compilation of legends grouped around a very ancient solar myth.

In the beginning, heaven and earth were not separate and formed a poorly-defined chaotic mass; the purest part broke away little by little and formed heaven. The rest "plunged down below" and eventually became earth. Then there appeared in "the plain of the upper skies" divinities (*kami*) which were born spontaneously. Five of them disappeared, no one knows how. After that, the seven divine generations followed one another. Among them, there was a god and his young sister—Izanagi, "the male who invites," and Izanami, "the female who invites." From their loves were born the eight great islands of Japan, then the six smaller ones.

Later, all the gods of nature were engendered, and finally, the god of fire who burned his mother so severely at the time of his delivery that she died. Izanagi, mad with grief, chops off the child's head, and the spilled blood is transformed into new divinities. Izanagi tries to snatch his wife from the land of shadows but fails. Returning to earth, he hastens to purify himself from the defilement he has just contracted. From each of the garments he takes off and from each part of his body which he bathes, twenty-six new divinities are born. Thus it happened that, finally, Amaterasu-o-mi-kami, goddess of the sun, was born from his life eye, Tsukiyomi-no-kami, the god of the moon, from his right eye, and from his nose, Take-haya-susanó-o-no-mikoto, god of the storm. Susano-o-no-mikoto does foolish things, is violent, knocks over the dikes in the ricefields, fills in the irrigation ditches, defiles the palace of his sister Amaterasu (goddess of the sun) who, outraged, hides in a cave whose entrance she seals off solidly by means of a huge rock.

Immediately, the world is plunged into darkness. The gods assemble. How will they make her come out? One of them makes a mirror, another a necklace, another, streamers of mulberry and hemp material. These objects are suspended from a camellia in front of the grotto. The goddess of laughter, Uzume, begins to dance. She dances with such spirit that she ends up removing her clothes. At this point the assembled gods burst into gales of laughter. Amaterasu, intrigued, puts her head out to find out what is behind all this uproar. She is handed the mirror in which she sees a goddess surpassing her in beauty. She comes forward to get a closer look and she is seized. A rope stretched in front of the cave prevents her from ever hiding in there again. Thus, she lights up the world again.

The sons of the god of wind are reigning over all of Japan, though Amaterasu had decided that her son would be the one to rule. To make such a complicated story short, her grandson will eventually govern to him she will entrust the three divine treasures symbolizing imperial power: the mirror, the piece of jewelry, and the saber. From this grandson of Amaterasu, goddess of the sun, springs Jimmutenno, the founder of the still-reigning imperial dynasty.

What is the origin of this myth of the sun concerning Amaterasu, the sun-goddess? That is a rather difficult question to answer. It is believed that a desire to give authenticity to the divine origin of the imperial family gave rise to the myth. The Japanese society of long ago was made up of clans, each of which had its tutelary god. The clan of the sun-god achieved a certain ascendancy over the others, and the myth of Amaterasu is supposed to have been made up later on to give a ring of authenticity to this supremacy of fact.

Before approaching the liturgy and worship of the Shinto religion, we must first discuss briefly the most outstanding characteristics of this religion which did so much to fashion the soul of Nippon.

Shintoism, as evidenced by this summary of the content of the faith, is a very primitive, inconsistent and vague religion, without metaphysics of any kind, without any element of speculation. Accordingly, it gives no precise information regarding the human soul, which it does not define. Moreover, no distinction between the soul and the body is established. The great problem of life and death is never broached.

This astonishing religion, at least in the beginning, did not have a system of morality in the Western sense. Later, under the influence of Buddhism, the concept of sin made its appearance in Shintoism. But sin was considered above all as a defilement, an obstacle to ritual purity, and not as a moral fault with reference to an interior moral law of conscience. For a Japanese, a sin is primarily an error, an error of strategy or tactics in reference to a law imposed from the outside (law of social life, law of the clan, ritualistic law of the sect, etc.). Every day, we Catholic priests have to struggle against this pharisaical formalism which is a real obstacle to the spiritual life of our neophytes.

However, to say that Shintoism has no morality system is a mistake. In spite of everything, we find in it a principle, that of *fidelity*, which can be, for us as missionaries, a springboard toward an authentic spiritual life. Fidelity to the nation, to the imperial family, to Japanese civilization, to the clan, to the laws of nature, to the given word. This very moving fidelity is one of the main virtues of the Japanese on which Shintoism is relying and which it is cultivating assiduously in the struggle against the wave of complete agnosticism of the younger generation.

In what does the Shintoist liturgy and its worship consist?

In the recitation of ritual prayers: the *norito*, sometimes very poetic, but easily understood. They are requests for graces (health, prosperity, harvest), but especially prayers expressing the gratitude and thankfulness of the faithful toward the gods. It is here that we find the vivacious, optimistic, gracious character of the Japanese people. But there is no place for personal prayer. Clapping the hands together and bowing for a second before a Shintoist sanctuary is in no way a religious experience, but merely the expression of a feeling of poetic communion with the past, with the roots of the people and the civilization of Japan.

In sacred dances: *kagura*, which recall the dance of Uzume in front of the cave in which Amaterasu, the goddess of the sun, had hidden herself. These dances are performed by very graceful young ladies; the poetic sentiment here again surpasses the religious experience.

In numerous ceremonies of ritual purification which are considered very important before any liturgical function. Water and salt play a large part in these purifications, along with branches of sakaki, the sacred tree of Japan, in the camellia family.

It will be noted how this concern for ritual purification (that is, external, having nothing to do with the sin which might stain a human conscience) is closely tied up with physical cleanliness, a major concern of the Japanese. Amid the diverse purification ceremonies, one must indicate fasting (*imi*), the ideal way of acquiring absolute purity by avoiding the very source of pollution. Here again we find this desire for divestment, for simplification, for frugality, which every Japanese feels deeply even if he does not heed it.

We must also point out various ceremonies and prayers to make a piece of land, the god of waters and springs, the winds, etc., favorable, and recognize clearly that the idea of sacrifice involving a renunciation does not exist in Shintoism. Offerings are made to the gods by way of thanksgiving, out of gratitude.

To round out this discussion of the Shinto cult, one should speak at great length about the famous festivals, the *Matsuri*, of Japan, which are in the process of becoming famous all over the world. These feasts of religious origin are also very characteristic of the Japanese spirit. The pretexts for celebrating a holiday are many: an offering to the gods as a sign of thanksgiving, the anniversary of the dedication of a temple, of an historical event, thanksgiving for the harvests, for the planting, etc. All these feasts invariably end up in extremely noisy processions, games, pantomimes, dances and drinking sprees, all of it very colorful, full of movement and jubilation.

Shintoism, which is a religious ritualism, does not have the slightest notion of a spiritual interior life, of an intimate dialogue between man and his God. The religious sentiment of Japan is always expressed in external, noisy, agitated rites, full of movement and always community-based.

Before concluding this too-brief overview of Shintoism, all that remains is to say a few words about the Shinto priests—the *kannushi*, their temples, the *jinja*, and finally, the worship of ancestors which, under the influence of Chinese Confucianism, has become grafted onto the trunk of the ancient, primitive, Shintoism.

The Shinto priesthood is hereditary. The Kannushi prays on the orders of and in the place of the Emperor, for the nation, for the people, for the health and prosperity of the Emperor himself. In this regard, it is very important to note that, while the Japanese affirm that their Emperor is god, and mean to adore him as such, the words "god" and "adoration" on their lips do not have the same meaning that we of the West, heirs of a Christian civilization, give them. *Kami* —"God"—is used also to designate the Emperor, the god of the sea, the hero dead in war, or simply, ancestors, the great-grandfather of some family. "To adore" also means to honor, to praise, as well as to venerate, and has no special relation to the adoration owed the absolute God.

Two things should be pointed out regarding the Shintoist priests. First of all, since Shintoism is no longer a state religion, since 1945, it receives no subsidy from the Government. Also, many priests practice a craft, often a liberal profession such as secondary school teaching. In addition, another problem, one concerning which the experts are quite divided, should be mentioned: is the Emperor the high priest of Shintoism? It would seem not. All the prayers said in the presence of the Emperor are offered in his name, the Emperor being content merely to attend. The court dress he puts on for the solemn great days (marriages, New Year holiday), while quite similar, is not the same as the liturgical garb of the Shinto priests, but is only the dress of the court of Nippon from time immemorial.

All visitors to Japan are unanimous in praising in numerous adjectives the very spare beauty of the Shinto temples, the *jinja*. In this vast architectural ensemble, the plane surfaces, the horizontal lines, the great esplanades, play a dominant role in imparting to the faithful a sense of the sanctity of the place and of the divine transcendence, without, however, abandoning that love of measure, of discretion, dear to the Japanese.

The sanctuary is a wooden edifice, raised, open-aired, in which historians see the primitive architecture of the Japanese house, of the "cabin" of the ancestors. In the center, there is the holy of holies where only the priest may enter. The prayers are read in front of the mirror, the saber and the jewelry, signs of the divinity, imperial insignia, entrusted of old by Amaterasu to her grandson.

One cannot leave Shintoism without saying a word about ancestor worship. Shintoism has often been defined as a religion of the ancestors, but this is incorrect. The cult of the deceased emperors developed under the influence of Confucianism which arrived in Japan in the 7th century. In the beginning, the Japanese did not devote a fervent piety to their ancestors. True, they had made a goddess into the ancestor of their Emperor. But this is altogether different from making gods of their ancestors!

But it was above all the philosopher Tchou-Hi (1130-1200 A.D.) and his theory on filial piety which had the greatest influence on Shintoism and the Japanese soul. Here is a definition of this doctrine according to Maspero: "Tchou-Hi's filial piety is not merely the natural feeling about the duties of children toward their parents; it is this feeling, to be sure, but cultivated, regulated, canalized in its expression and extended to the entire moral life. The action of filial piety goes beyond the horizon of the family in all directions; it extends to the relations of inferiors with superiors, of subjects with sovereigns, and even, in general, of men among themselves, for 'whoever loves his parents, dares not hate his neighbor; whoever honors his parents, dares not be insolent toward his neighbor'; it reaches its supreme peak in self-perfection."

Even in our own time the Japanese soul remains deeply marked by this Confucian thinking, along with all social relations: teachers and students, masters and servants, workers and bosses. The class struggle has no meaning in this mentality, and God knows what a tremendous effort of destruction is being made by the Marxists in Japan in order to create this struggle and this hatred.

* * *

II. *Buddhism*

At this point, we approach Japanese Buddhism which, together with the original Shintoism and Confucianism, has been a dominant factor in the formation of the Japanese soul.

Everyone is familiar with the problem that tortured the mind of the Indian sage Sakya-Muni, around the year 573 B.C. Why does man suffer? And everyone knows of the illumination of the saint and of his reply: it is the illusion of the self, the desire "to be," to continue to "be," the thirst to live into the beyond, which causes our suffering and forces us to be re-born indefinitely. (The doctrine of transmigration of souls is prior to Buddhism; perhaps it came from Vedism?) Let us recognize that our ego has no existence, let us suppress it by loving all beings and all things, and we shall be happy. We will be able to free ourselves from the necessity of being re-born; we will leave the path of transmigration and enter into unconditional life, into nirvana.

This doctrine divided with the passage of time into two great currents:

The Small Vehicle—Hînayâna. A pessimistic and misanthropic doctrine which encourages the neglect of daily life to achieve the only Truth, to attain salvation primarily for oneself.

The Grand Vehicle—Mahâyâna, which is more optimistic and goes further. Not only must one save oneself, but, in order to arrive at the state of Buddha (the illuminated), it is necessary to save all living beings. To do this, the actions of daily life suffice.

It was this concern for helping to save others which led a large number of famous personages to come out of the shadows and teach salvation, Sakya-Muni himself (Shaka Sama in Japanese), the personified aspect of eternal wisdom, being but one figure in the cosmic, unending procession of supernatural beings.

Introduction of Buddhism to Japan

In 523 A.D., Buddhism arrived in Japan for the first time. A Korean delegation heartily recommended Buddhism to the Emperor Kemmi Tenno as a new religion, and brought him a statue of Buddha as a gift. The Emperor's advisers were at first skeptical. The Soga clan came out in favor of a trial; the Monobe clan stood firm against this innovation. Then a terrible epidemic arose. The statue of the unknown god was blamed and was thrown into the river. The Imperial palace burned down. The terrified Emperor had two statues made, and the clan of the Soga, which saw in the religious question a good opportunity to supplant the opposing camp, supported Buddhism with all its strength against the Monobe clan. The Soga clan was triumphant. One of the sons of the Emperor (a Soga), Shotoku-Taishi, became a fervent

Buddhist and in 587, Buddhism was officially permitted throughout the Empire.

Triumph of Buddhism in Japan

It is true that the year 587 marked the triumph of Buddhism, but the full flourishing was not until the 8th century A.D., during the Nara period, when the Emperor Shomu-Tenno, like Shotoku Taishi, protected Buddhism and through it, sought to increase his people's happiness. Buddhism and the state formed an alliance. The Emperor had the great Buddha (Daibutsu) of Nara built, and in 741 gave the order to found in each province a temple with a community of 20 bonzes and a pagoda with 10 nuns, commissioned to pray, to read the sutras and to fast, in order to protect the country not only from calamities, but from immorality itself!

The era of Nara therefore, witnessed the triumph of Buddhism in Japan. Still, it was at that point only a religion of the elite. To the masses, it was a foreign religion about which they knew nothing. The people remained attached to the native religion, and sometimes even showed a certain animosity toward these new gods—all the more so because the diversity of the numerous Buddhist sects added to the confusion.

It was the glory of the Buddhist monk Gyogi (670-749 A.D.) to cause Buddhism to be accepted by everybody, by demonstrating through a bold syncretism that Buddhism and Shintoism were two currents of one and the same religion. The problem was this: how to assimilate Buddhism while preserving Shinto as the national religion. Gyogi's solution was to bring the Shinto divinities into the Buddhist pantheon and to call the new religion *Ryobu shinto*: two-current Shinto. Gyogi, in effect, taught that Buddhism and Shintoism were but two different forms of one same faith, and that the national deities were but "phases," "manifestations," of the Buddhist divinities.

In this way, Buddhism not only brought the Shintoist divinities into its pantheon, but also gave them an external form, made idols of them while carefully presenting them as national manifestations of the eternal Buddha. The supreme accomplishment, finally, was to declare that Buddha and Amaterasu are identical. It was an elegant way for Buddhism to monopolize her great-grandsons, the Mikados!

Profound reasons for the triumph of Buddhism in Japan

Before going on with our study of Japanese Buddhism, we must try to understand the reasons which impelled the Japanese to adopt Buddhism so quickly and so thoroughly.

One of the primordial qualities of the Japanese people is unquestionably its proverbial curiosity, its intellectual ferment, still just as lively today. In the 8th century, the Japanese were already aspiring to progress in all fields, both spiritual and material. They already wished to assimilate foreign civilizations: Shotoku Taishi is a good example of this. Not only did he protect Buddhism, as we have seen, but, trained by a Confucianist teacher, he had certain principles of Confucius adopted in his code of 604 A.D.

This idea of the Japanese—that to adopt a civilization is to adopt its moral system and its religion as well—did much for the triumph of Buddhism. This did not take place at the time of the reform of *Meiji* in the 19th century. The Japanese of that period no doubt did not have a very exalted idea of the religion of the Europeans from what they saw of it in the concrete! It must be said, to our relief, unfortunately, that in the 8th century, Shinto was unable to satisfy the religious aspirations of the nation's elite, because it was far too much under the influence of the clans as a means of oppression to preserve the privileges of the castes. For many people, Buddhism became an excellent means of escaping the tyranny of the clan.

The narrow ritualism of Shintoism also favored the triumph of the foreign religion which brought to minds thirsting for the absolute, the great idea that virtue is rewarded, and that Paradise is the goal of human life. The Japanese, who have always been so delicate in their feelings, were moreover happy to know that it was necessary to pray for the dead in order to obtain well-being for them in the after-life, an ideal way of expressing one's gratitude to those who worked so hard for us during this life. Thus it was that the construction of temples and monasteries charged with guaranteeing prayers for the deceased was immediately undertaken, at great expense. Certainly, all the Japanese of that time could hardly have had strong arguments regarding the usefulness of Buddhism in the work of universal salvation, but each of them was very much aware that he had there, at his disposal, a practical means of insuring his own well-being, primarily material, thanks to the quasi-magical power which the bonzes imparted to the sutras and to the different ceremonies of the cult.

The missionary bonzes, moreover, did not fail to stress this magical and superstitious side in their discourses to the good country folk—for there were indeed real missions organized through the different areas of the country. But while the missionaries were zealous, they were never combative or provoking, something the Japanese always abhor.

Finally, one of the most powerful means for developing Buddhism was the establishment of schools near every temple. Buddhism practically had a monopoly on education and, in addition, every bonze was filled with the idea that he was obliged not only to make the people benefit from his knowledge, but also to make them benefit from all his wealth, spiritual as well as material.

Japanese Buddhism beginning with the 8th Century

The era of Nara saw the triumph of Buddhism. However, despite Gyogi's effort at syncretism, it still remained a religion of the elite, a foreign religion imported from China.

It was not until the era of Heian (9th-12th centuries, A.D.), through a new effort of assimilation to adapt the Indo-Chinese civilization to the circumstances and the temperament of Japan, that Buddhism really became a popular Japanese religion. This assimilation effort would bear fruit and the new graft would cause the ancient trunk of the Japanese civilization to flourish again. Buddhism would become Japanese, and there would even be Japanese theologians who would do the work of innovators.

During the 9th century, the government sought to escape the domination of the Buddhist clergy and the intrigues of politicians and military men; it moved the capital from Nara to Kyoto (Heian). Buddhism took advantage of this change of capitals in the sense that it breathed in fresh air and tried to put itself within the reach of the people and to respond to their spiritual needs. On the one hand, syncretism was further stressed and perfected. On the other, the development of Japanese script (*kana*, a 96-symbol alphabet) facilitated the democratization of Buddhism. From that time on, everyone could read the holy books. Where formerly these books had been written in Chinese characters, now all the great founders of sects during the Heian age used this Japanese alphabet in their popularizing works.

This democratization, above all this "Japan-ization" of Buddhism was to be the task of three sects—*Tendai, Shingon, Jodoshu*—from which almost all the modern sects are derived. All three were reactions against the aristocratic nature of the Nara Buddhism. The characteristic feature of these three new sects was their attitude toward man: everyone can become a Buddhist, not just the initiated or the perfect. Here we find a concern for egalitarianism which clearly reflects one aspect of Japanese thinking.

The Tendai Sect. Its founder, Dengyo Daishi (752-822 A.D.), taught absolute monism: all is "thought" and thought is "Buddha." The following parable, called the "parable of the mirror," is a good representation not only of the Tendai doctrine, but also of its characteristic teaching method:

"The radiating of the mirror belongs to the first form of existence: the *ku*, that is, the void, the nothing, the emptiness. The objects reflected by the mirror are part of the second form of existence: the *ka*, that is, the "contingent." The mirror itself is *chu*, that is, "that which is in the middle," the "substance." These three elements do not exist in isolation. Even the mirror, without light and the objects which it reflects, ceases to be a mirror. *Ku-Ka-Chu* only exist as a system of relation to a whole. Thus, in the universe, nothing can subsist separated from the whole, nor can the whole subsist without the infinite complexities woven of emptiness and contingency." (according to Fosco Maraini)

The consequences of such a doctrine are of tremendous importance. First of all, Buddhist salvation is *universal:* men, beasts, plants and things, all and everything, being of a common Buddhist essence, can become Buddha. Then, and this is the essential point, the *infinite value* of man and things is clearly affirmed. Here we are touching directly on the immense goodness of the Buddhist believer toward all creatures, regardless of what they may be. And, it must be said, we are face to face with an authentic *humanism* capable of bringing down our Christian humanism, if we are not careful. For a Japanese pragmatist, the only possible difference between these two humanisms will be this: does the Christian live his doctrine? does the Buddhist do what his faith commands him? We Christians are judged on our degree of effective love—a frightening responsibility.

The Shingon sect. Kobo-Daishi (774-835 A.D.), said to be the inventor of the Japanese alphabet, also taught absolute monism. But his method of presenting his doctrine was such that he had a great influence on Japanese "folklore" (if I may use that word).

The universe, whose essence is Buddha, presents two aspects: the exoteric and the esoteric. According to Kobo-Daishi, all the other sects studied only the exoteric explanations of the universe. Only the Shingon sect goes further and opens up to us the esoteric views of the universe wherein resides, in its absolute purity, the profound "thought" of Buddha, and thus gives us access to fundamental "reality."

The world thinks and speaks to us. We must know how to grasp its message, how to reserve to ourselves, through purity of heart, an interior sanctuary to hear the far-off echo of the message of the Buddha. Thus to understand the esoteric meaning of the world is to be Buddha.

Therefore, in the universe, everything is a symbol, everything has a hidden meaning. Worship in the Shingon sect consists in unrestrained symbolism: gods, demi-gods, titans, heroes, geniuses, celestial powers, mysterious things and forces of the world, all become heavenly persons bearing a "message." Every gesture, every attitude, is an invocation of Buddha, a "union" with him. Whence the importance of the liturgy, of the architecture of the sanctuary, of the statuary, of the sacred texts, of the attitudes to be assumed to meditate, of chanting, of sacred music, etc. Fosco Maraini points out very effectively that the Shingon sect is "an esoteric religion which is nourished by sighs, secrets, the subtle intoxication of the senses, combined with an extreme penetration of the spirit."

It is unnecessary to stress that a Japanese, steeped in this sense of the sacred, accustomed from childhood to the most subtle symbols, is quite at home in our Catholic liturgy. The very sober Roman liturgy, Gregorian chant, the Sacraments and the sacramentals, all enrapture him once the general meaning of the ceremonies has been pointed out to him.

The Jodo Shu sect. During the second half of the 11th century and throughout the 12th, decadence set in all social classes. Among the rulers, in the aristocracy, among the religious, immorality spread until it constituted a social danger.

Faced with this sad spectacle, certain "sages" sought solitude by becoming hermits; others, on the contrary, tried to propagate the faith among the masses by experimenting with some new teaching methods. Among these ardent souls, Genshin (942-1017), of the Tendai sect, taught the efficacy of prayer in one of his famous books: *Essential Elements of Salvation. Ojo Yoshu* did the same. *Enko Daishi* (1133-1212), also known as Honen, took up these same teachings and founded the very famous sect of *Jodo Shu*—the "sect of the pure earth," which preaches the worship of *Amida*, "lord of the infinite light" and the recitation of the invocation: *Namu Amida Butsu,* or "homage to the Buddha Amida."

On his death-bed, Enko Daishi himself set forth his beliefs very clearly:

> "The method of final salvation which I have taught is not a sort of meditation such as that practiced by many wise men in China and in Japan in the past, nor the repetition of the names of Buddha by those who have studied and understood his profound significance. It is nothing more than the simple repetition of the name of the Buddha Amida, without the slightest doubt of his mercy, through which one has access to the land of perfect happiness."

The consequences of this doctrine were also important in the formation of the Japanese soul.

First of all, a true theism replaced absolute monism. Then, with the affirmation of the total efficacy of the *nem butsu* (repetition of a formula), salvation was open to the simple man, for whom the instruction or the reading of the sacred works of the other sects had been impossible. Finally, and this was the most serious part, the prayers of the bonzes, the temples, the hierarchy, became useless. An independent church without priests or ceremonies was established. This was the signal for a veritable religious war. Enko Daishi was exiled for a time, and some of his disciples were beheaded.

Shinran Shonin (1174-1268), of the Tendai sect, then of the Jodo Shu sect, took up the doctrine of Enko Daishi and pushed it to the extreme, affirming the exclusive efficacy of the formula *Namu Amida Butsu.* This amounted to proclaiming the absolute necessity of faith without works. To be saved, one needs only simple little every-day morality. Even a single invocation, recited with faith, just once in a lifetime, suffices. Of course, other invocations are useful, but merely as additional homage to the Buddha Amida.

Shinran Shonin organized his own sect, *Jodo Shin Shu,* the "new sect of the pure earth," open to all, especially the humble, and in which everyone, regardless of origin, was treated on the same equal footing. This sect became one of the most flourishing in Japan, and still is today. The famous and magnificent temples of Kyoto—Honganji and Higashi-Honganji, belong to this sect.

But in practice many of the faithful of the sect realized that the famous sacred formula *Namu Amida Butsu* did not possess the effectiveness attributed to it. While all recite it with fervor or at least out of habit, it often happens that people will say, regarding some big lazy character just loafing around: "He is like the sacred formula, good-for-nothing!"

Before concluding this rapid overview of Japanese Buddhism, we really must say something about two other more recent sects which have also had considerable influence in the forming of the Japanese spirit: *Nichiren Shu* and *Zen Shu.*

The Nichiren sect. At the end of the 11th century and during most of the 12th century, the disorders of the second half of the so-called *Heian* period, continued. The imperial court remained at Heian, but the *Bafuku* administration installed itself at Kamakura, and the Shogunate stripped the Emperor of most of his powers, while generously leaving him the sovereignty. What occurred, therefore, was not only the decline of the patrician society, but the social disintegration of the country. The corruption of the clergy, well-provided with benefices, was a scandal. Naturally, this disintegration was matched by a corresponding elevation of the military class, which acquired new national importance in the struggle against the Mongols. Among the little people, this disintegration was met by a corresponding rebirth of religious fervor. As a reaction to the end of the Heian era, there was a return to the old sects of the Nara period, and the birth of new sects animated by a violently reformist spirit.

The monk Nichiren (1222-1282), was certainly the man most representative of this reforming spirit. But, and this is characteristic of such a troubled age, Nichiren was as much a political reformer as a religious reformer, inspired as he was by a very strong national spirit. He fought first of all against the other sects, which he found too numerous. He saw in them a danger, in that, since they divided the faithful up among themselves, they were breaking up the national unity and sapping the vitality of the Japanese people. And this, according to him, was the principal cause of the corruption of the state.

His religious teachings consisted almost solely in the teaching of the holy book, the sutra *Myoho-Rengekyo*—"book of the lotus of the good law." In these days of decadence, thought Nichiren, the path of salvation must be simple. The simple repetition of a formula containing the statement of the three mysteries and the three esoteric principles of the world would be enough: *Namu Myoho Rengekyo*, "honor to the lotus of the good law!" According to him, these mechanical repetitions of the same formula must be as so many pieces of the Truth. The identity of essence of Buddhist spiritual things means that the truth has two faces: the inexpressible and the expressed. The aspect of the second face, which enables the most ignorant of men to participate in the work of salvation, does not change the basis, which is the light of the Buddha.

Thus we find again in Nichiren the same teachings as in

the other great founders of sects: the same esoterism, the same sense of the divine immanence, the same humanism, the same love of the little man and of his salvation. But this antagonism toward the other sects, this radical intolerance, the intransigent nationalism, mean that the Nichiren sect appears to the Japanese as a sect of fanatics which is attractive yet slightly frightening. It is public knowledge among Japanese Catholics that a faithful member of the Nichiren sect could only be converted with great difficulty.

The Zen sect. The reaction against the formalistic Buddhism of the Heian period found concrete expression in a return to the life of the old sects of the Nara age, and in the birth of new antagonistic sects, as we pointed out, among which was the Nichiren sect.

During the same period, the resurrection and elevation of the Zen sect shared in the same state of mind.

The teachings of the three sects, Jodo Shu, Jodo Shin Shu and Nichiren Shu, can be considered identical. In effect, each of these sects places the reality of salvation in the recitation of a formula. But the Zen sect teaches a different means of obtaining salvation. No longer is it a question of a formula, but of interior illumination. Salvation is attained by a direct intuition, the fruit of the effort of the man who, by voluntarily detaching himself from the created, grasps the meaning of the universe.

Steinilber-Oberlin quotes a bonze on the subject of this doctrine which is so difficult to express in words:

> "I will tell you of the origin of Zenism. One day, Buddha took a lotus in his hand, looked at the flower, then smiled without saying a word. None of his disciples understood what this smile meant, except one, his favorite

> pupil, who looked at his master and smiled too. The two of them, in silence, had understood one another. Do not ask what this smile meant . . . no one could tell you . . . I look upon explanations the way a wise Chinese used to look upon translations: 'they are brocades examined from the wrong side: the threads, the colors are the same, but the essential is no longer there.' Zen thinking is transmitted without the help of texts or words; this is why it is called: 'the doctrine of thought transmitted by thought.' Through an intuitive, personal, original, non-communicable effort, seek in yourself your own authenticity. Each of us bears a Buddha in himself; he must be discovered. He waits for you; seek him out, and smile at him."

Illumination, the goal of the Zenists' efforts, is called in Japanese *satori*, that is, "comprehension," the fruit of an intimate personal experience.

This is how Steinilber-Oberlin defines this *satori*: "an intuitive look into the very nature of things, as opposed to the logical comprehension of the latter. Practically speaking, this signifies the revelation of a new world heretofore unnoticed in the confusion of our dualistic spirit."

It is quite obvious that a degree of asceticism, of liberation from self, from the created world, is necessary. This also presupposes total spiritual concentration and purity of life, an authentic poverty—the material condition for moral independence and the development of intuitive qualities.

At the end of this study of some of the great Zen principles, a question spontaneously comes to mind: "Christianity seems very close to certain Zen teachings, particularly those regarding the use of created goods. Would it not therefore be easy for a faithful Zenist to adhere to Christianity?

Is not Zen a stepping-stone for Christianity in the heart of the Japanese world?" Unfortunately not. This is what a Professor of Buddhism in a Kyoto university writes concerning the fundamental difference between Christianity and Zenism (quoted by Steinilber-Oberlin):

> "When Christ said: 'Let not your left hand know what the right hand is doing,' this is similar to the secret virtue of Buddhism. But when he adds: 'your Father who sees you, though you do not see him, will reward you,' Buddhism and Christianity go separate ways. So long as you believe that someone, God or devil, has seen you do good, Zen says to you, 'you are not one of ours.' That is not 'action without merit': it has left traces and marks. The perfect garment has no seams. We expect nothing, either from our own conscience, or from a God . . . The mind must be purified from all that the centuries have accumulated. Then it appears without garments, naked, empty, free and sincere. Then it re-discovers its original force. And that too is joy, a joy from which nothing can be taken away, to which nothing can be added. No doubt all mystiques are looking for a similar goal, but in Christianity, the faithful is still too aware of a God."

It is clearly superfluous to stress the inadequacy of such a mystique without God, limited to our human horizons only. But it is undeniable that Zen has awakened among the Japanese virtues and a strength of soul which are rare indeed. The military class especially has been influenced by this doctrine of renunciation and of self-mastery. *Bushido*, the honor code of chivalry, is completely permeated with it —stoic bearing of trials, disdain for wealth and death, separation from everything that is mean or has the aroma of self-interest.

We have come to the end of our study of the principal religious currents in Japan, and the feeling distilled from it seems to be as follows:

Shintoism, along with the various Buddhist sects, represent a genuine and sincere effort to discover the truth about man and his destiny. But this human search, however moving it may be, remains limited to our human horizons and seems incapable of rising above them, toward the contemplation of a personal God, the savior of man and his friend. In this regard, the "sacred books" of Christianity, by their content of divine revelation, are the only ones capable of raising man above himself and of teaching him the way that leads to the Savior-God.

In addition, this semi-solution to the human problem offered by "Buddhist humanism," through its love—sincere to be sure, but closed—of man, through its religiosity without real theological foundation, seems to be a serious obstacle to the progress of Christianity. His heart full of pity for man and for all creatures, his thirst for the absolute and the sacred slaked by the traditional magic rites, the faithful Buddhist sees no reason to go in search somewhere else for a truth he does not suspect. Saturated for centuries with theological quarrels among the various sects, our Japanese Buddhist long ago resigned himself to religious relativism, and, in view of the "life insurance" for the Beyond contracted for in good and proper form by certain ritual acts, considers himself the happiest of men!

7. R. P. DEMANN | JUDAISM

For some people, a Jew is first of all "he who still awaits the Messias." In general, Judaism is very poorly understood. Thus, for example, two years ago, during a meeting held in Basel for Catholic, Protestant and Jewish theologians on the problem of salvation, the majority of the Protestants and Catholics seemed astounded to find themselves facing interlocutors who were not exactly what they expected. They discovered that, like Christianity, Judaism had developed over nineteen centuries. This ignorance of Judaism is explained by history, but it is nonetheless regrettable.

Since the time of Jesus Christ, the two communities have developed alongside one another. There was a double evolution, at once parallel and opposed. During the first centuries of Christianity, the two communities evolved by continuously positioning themselves in relation to one another, but then they separated to the point of almost ignoring one another completely. A dialogue thus became extremely difficult. Today, it takes a large effort, with facts and openness of mind, for a Christian who wants to understand Judaism from the inside, and vice versa.

The effort must be greater for the Christians, for the Jews have lived in a Christian environment and therefore have at their disposal numerous facts and sources of information, whereas we are ignorant of practically the entire life and history of the Jews since Jesus Christ, and do not always have the means of learning about them.

For centuries, then, the effort at understanding had become non-existent and almost impossible. It is only in the last century and a half, thanks to the civil and social emancipation of the Jews, that contact and dialogue have again become possible. During the last several decades, and particularly since the last war, the conscience of the Christian world has awakened to the Jewish problem.

The Jewish world is vast and presents multiple aspects: religious, sociological, ethnic, historical. We shall limit ourselves here to the study of the Jewish religion.

First of all, we must take care not to judge Judaism on the basis of all the Jews we may meet. There is only a small minority which realizes, reflects, and expresses precisely just what Judaism is as a religion, just as only a small minority of Christians reflects what Christianity is.

What is Judaism?

We shall assume a certain knowledge of the Jewish religion prior to Jesus Christ, in order to limit ourselves to post-biblical and present-day Judaism. However, Christ does not constitute a cut-off point in Judaism. After the exile period, Judaism organized itself with its synagogues and its Scriptures in the form which has remained substantially the same down to the present.

Judaism is above all a monotheistic religion, characterized by faith in a living God, the creator, the God of history, who has a plan of salvation, of love and of mercy for the world. Man's sin is a resistance to this plan. To carry out His design, God chose instruments for Himself: a people, to whom He gave a central role in the history of salvation, and an expression of His will, which became the Torah and which would guide the people in their mission.

Since the time of post-exile Judaism, a vision of history, with Sinai at its center, has been sketched out. It was there, on Sinai, that God gave Israel its structure, its law. The Covenant established the chosen people. To understand the essential place of this event in the life of Judaism, we must stress that Judaism is a religion linked to a people—not a people in the ethnic sense of the word, but a community formed by a cohesion of solidarity in the same destiny. This feeling is so strong in the Jewish world that some part of it is found even among those Jews most detached from the Tradition.

The whole faith of Israel is tied in with the events of Sinai: only that which was revealed to Moses is Revelation, given in a bloc on Sinai. The rest is but commentary. Scripture and living Tradition play as essential a role as in Christianity, Scripture being but a privileged moment in the oral and living Tradition. The living Tradition is also tied to Sinai, to Moses. It seeks to keep the Revelation of the Pentateuch, the Torah, ever present. Jewish Tradition is formed around the Scriptures, without separating itself from them.

This central role of the Torah is found again in the Jewish liturgy. In ancient Judaism, there was a sacrificial liturgy, centered in the Temple of Jerusalem, but its importance quickly decreased. At the time of the Exile, a second form of worship was established and persisted after the destruction of the second Temple of Jerusalem and the disappearance of the sacrificial liturgy, in 70 A.D.

The liturgy of the synagogue has a structure analogous to our pre-Mass or Mass of the Catechumens. At the heart of each service, there is the reading of a passage from the Pentateuch and an excerpt from the Prophets matched to the first reading, all of it surrounded by blessings and prayers drawn in large part from the Psalter. The whole liturgy testifies to the importance of the Covenant of Sinai. This Covenant is the prototype of the divine intervention. Only one event will have an equal importance: the final Coming. The Messias is thought of as a second Moses: Moses laid the foundations for this coming, and the Messias will come when Israel has accomplished its mission.

Israel bears witness by faithfully fulfilling the will of God, His Law. Thus, today as 2000 years ago, the life of the faithful Jew is conceived as a living testimony given before the world, a constant testimony which must hasten the coming of God's Kingdom. The observances and prayer enclose in a kind of network the entire life of the Jew, in which there is no more separation between profane and sacred: blessings sanctify every action. This is one of the most beautiful, the most profound, the most winning things about Judaism, but also one of the most difficult aspects of it to carry out, for this religious life can only be completely implemented in a community organized in terms of it.

We have emphasized the central role of the events on Sinai. Judaism, however, is not turned toward the past. It actualizes the past in the present. Every time a Jew sanctifies some action or other in observance of the Torah, he is accomplishing the Covenant. Thus, the Covenant is unceasingly renewed. Later events are prepared for in the sanctification of present events. This eschatological movement is simpler than for us, as Christians, for whom salvation was acquired by Christ who "has come and is to come again," yet is still awaited. For Judaism, history has two poles: Sinai and the coming of the Kingdom. And in the important prayers, there is always a reference to the Covenant, to the past ("Blessed art Thou, God of our Fathers, God of Abraham, of Isaac . . ."), and to the future ("Blessed art Thou, O Eternal One who dost vivify the dead"). Israel must remain faithful. Every time a Jew strays from the Law, the coming of the Kingdom is delayed.

Does the mission of the Jewish people have a universal character?

For the Jews themselves, the reply to this is not very clear-cut. Judaism has never lost the sense of this universalism, but has never completely expressed it. Because it was always confined to one people, Judaism could not go beyond a certain particularism. The problem of universalism concerns Jewish thinkers. For instance, regarding the time of the Kingdom, if one asks Jews: "Will there be a difference between Israel and the others?" some will answer "yes" and others "no," and there is no way to settle the debate definitively. The Law which defines all aspects of Jewish life sets Israel apart; this setting apart is God's wish. In our Christian perspective, this setting apart has been by-passed, but for the Jews it has not. In this sense, today's Judaism is similar to the Judaism of Christ's time.

Here we are touching upon the problem of the origin of the conflict with Christianity. The break came in large measure over the question of maintaining the legal and national framework of God's People. There was a conflict within the apostolic community itself, between Paul and the "Judaizers." And a situation swiftly developed in which the Christians reproached the Jews for refusing Christ, and the Jews reproached the Christians for refusing the Law.

Who is Christ for the Jews?

After the first centuries, the Jews, for most of the Middle Ages, were pushed into a defensive position. They turned fatally into themselves, lived in closed communities, practically speaking ignorant of Christ. Christianity, or more accurately, Christendom, became in their eyes primarily the persecutor who hid Christ completely from them. The question did not come up again until after the emancipation of the Jews. Since that time, a very diversified evolution has been taking shape, and is leading to new positions.

Some, then, go as far as conversion (few). Others go as far as to believe in Christ, without being able to accept the Church. Others read the Gospel and admire Christ, but go no further.

There has also been a whole current of thought regarding Christ, about which one cannot speak without knowing the historical context. The years between 1830 and 1860 were the golden age of liberal Protestant exegesis, which eliminated the divinity of Christ and the transcendence of Christianity. The Jews found greater sympathy on the part of Protestants than of Catholics. From liberal Protestantism, they were able to accept Jesus, considered as a good Jew who practiced the Law and did not call Himself God. For them, it was not Jesus who effected the rupture, it was Paul, who divinized Christ and created the Church. The break was no longer between Jesus and Judaism, but between Paul and Jesus. This thinking led to a rather coherent synthesis of the

New Testament: what concerns Jesus, great rabbi, great moralist, but purely human, is authentic; but that which affirms Jesus-God is due to the Paulinian, even the pagan, influence.

In the United States some liberal Jews even consider Jesus as a prophet.

What is the position of Judaism with regard to the Christian fact?

Ever since the 10th and 11th centuries, Jewish thinkers have questioned themselves about the success of Christianity and of Islam, and have managed to give this explanation of it: "Judaism is a very demanding religion and the Law was given to Israel alone. Therefore, Providence raised up Christianity and Islam as adaptations of the message of Israel for the use of the 'Gentiles,' without imposing the whole Law and observances on them." This view made it possible to explain the cessation of Jewish proselytism, which was very considerable after the Exile, at the time of the hellenistic Judaism, and which still existed at the beginning of the Middle Ages.

We have seen that Judaism is a religion difficult to live in an integrated way in a non-Jewish world. From the 4th century A.D. down to the French Revolution, the Jews were apart from the life of society in Christian lands. Suddenly, they found themselves plunged into it and since then, the problem has arisen of adapting the religion to modern life. Up to that time, there had been a single tradition, and this great unity was maintained thanks to the authorities and books recognized by everyone.

During the Middle Ages, and until the emancipation, various mystical or doctrinal tendencies had only involved the formation of opposing tendencies or schools, just as differences of language and culture gave rise to liturgical diversification (Sephardic liturgy in Spain, Ashkenazi liturgy in Central Europe, etc.). But the emancipation of the Jews brought with it a profound though not essential rupture of unity. Today, speaking in terms of sentiment, there is but one Judaism; from the religious point of view, at least three main forms of it can be distinguished:

a) Orthodox Judaism, which tries to keep the whole Tradition, regardless of the difficulties encountered in the modern world.
b) In contrast, Reform (or liberal or progressive) Judaism, which attempts, boldly, openly, to bring about a reform. In order to save and revivify the essentials of the Tradition, it advocates an evolution, an adaptation of the liturgy, of the observances, of the life of the communities.
c) Between these two, Conservative Judaism tries to keep not only the substance of the Tradition, but the greatest share possible of the traditional forms of the teaching and practice of Judaism, while seeking to adapt them not only on the level of the observances, but also on the level of thought (for example, by taking into account modern biblical exegesis).

But there is no longer any authority which all would accept as absolutely as in former days. Judaism is broken in its unity, like the Christian world, with this difference, that it retains, on a different level, a far stronger cohesion and solidarity.

In the United States, out of five and a half million Jews, about half belong to a community and are divided in about equal proportions among the three forms of Judaism.

In France, the "official" consistorial Judaism is a Conservative Judaism. Nevertheless, there are numerous small orthodox communities and a few reform communities (among them, one in Paris, relatively unimportant numerically, but very active).

Judaism in Israel constitutes a very special case. Only Orthodox Judaism exists there officially and in an organized manner. But, in reality, there is a veritable ferment of multiple tendencies and searchings. The present population of Israel is very young: 50 per cent is under twenty years of age. Whence a very rapid evolution of ideas, among which certain constants are beginning to stand out. There is a great difference between those over forty and the young. Among those over forty, there is a small minority of unbelievers, 15 to 20 per cent are strict Orthodox Jews, and a large mass, without practicing everything, retain a certain faith (sometimes very lively) and certain religious practices. Among the young, there is a polarization toward the two extremes: a return to a more complete practice, or a more thorough abandonment. In general, the problem of religion is a matter of concern, and attempts are being made to solve it.

More and more, one has the impression of the extreme unadaptability of the institutions and the representatives of Israel's official Orthodoxy to modern life, and the young people seem to be opposed to this orthodoxy and to the religious policies to which it inspires its representatives.

But, certain indications make it possible to discern an interesting evolution among orthodox youth themselves. Throughout the population, and especially the young people, the biblical impregnation is very strong: culture, language, country. This impregnation seems to create in the young a spiritual exigency manifested in nostalgia for a return to a

Judaism closer to biblical Judaism, less institutional, more prophetic.

But, to be sure, these are as yet only aspirations, a groping search, in a world in ferment.

8. GASTON FESSARD, S.J. | CONTEMPORARY ATHEISM

In contemporary atheism, different currents of thought can be distinguished: Sartre, Merleau-Ponty, Camus . . . but only one, Marxism, has given rise to a religion. In Communism, as a matter of fact, we have a veritable religion, certainly important both because of the number of its true practitioners and because of their quality.

This is a common truth. Berdyaev, a socialist student under the Czar, was the first to formulate it. Deported to Siberia, then, after the Revolution of 1917, a Professor of Marxism, he was expelled at the end of two years, emigrating to Germany and finally, to France, where he published books that were a revelation about Russian Communism. In particular, he declared: "Communism is an inverse theocracy."

Guided by this Russian philosopher, Maritain speaks of an "earthly religion"; Raymond Aron, of a "secular religion." Madeleine Delbrel, in *Marxist City, a Mission Land*, published by Les Editions du Cerf in 1958, affirmed the same thing. For 25 years a militant Christian in Ivry, "the French Rome of Marxism," she had many Communist friends. On the basis of the contacts and conversations she was able to have there she wrote in her book: "Marxism is religiously atheistic. These two words are only compatible in the absurd. Marxism is willing to be absurd in order to take advantage of their striking contradiction, through which it can dazzle man's religious sense, turn it completely inside out, recover its energies freed of all alienation for purposes where their inspiration is lacking. Man, for his part, will not feel frustrated; even his religious aptitudes will be exploited, he will be at peak capacity. . . . Marxism is built on a faith which is not only religious, but founded on a revelation." Even as a religion, Marxism defends its bases and intends to be unassailable. It is nearly impossible to preserve oneself from its atheism unless one knows its source, unless one knows why it became a religion.

I. *The atheistic background of Marxism*

First of all, a general comment. In approaching Marxism, one must rid oneself of any inferiority complex. "People have spoken," says Madeleine Delbrel, "of the influence of Marxism on inadequately prepared Christians. There is less said concerning the indirect influence of Marxism as a 'fact,' as the organizer of half of the world. Its very size causes a kind of inferiority complex among the masses of Christians, incoherent, like all complexes. It is this complex one finds at the root of the half-truths . . ." In fact, it is among the Christian elites, among the intellectuals, that this inferiority complex does the most damage. On the contrary, one must take pride in one's Christian faith, whose dimensions are extraordinarily greater. But pride does not mean presumption, for Marxism cannot be conquered without an effort of intellect and thought equal to that which gave birth to this movement. On that condition, faith makes it possible, then, to go beyond Marxism without harm.

Where does Communism obtain its dimension as an atheistic religion? Marxism is defined as "historical and dialectical materialism," and claims that it borrowed its method, which united theory and practice, from the doctrines of Hegel. Lenin has written: "It is impossible to understand Marx' *Das Kapital* without having studied and understood all of Hegel's *Logic*. Thus, no Marxist has understood Marx a half century after him."[1] Moreover, Hegel's dialectics remained very obscure even for Lenin, who only notes the concrete examples, such as the law of the passage of quality into quantity (water-steam) etc., and declares "obscure," "very obscure," their dialectical explanations. To understand Hegel, it is necessary to study above all his *The Phenomenology of the Spirit* (translated by Hippolyte), with various commentaries, among them, those of the Russian A. Kojev.

Hegel, born in 1770, ended his career as Professor of Philosophy at the University of Berlin. He died in 1831. A roommate in 1794 of Schelling and Hölderlin at the Protestant Seminary at Tübingen, he had been at that time among the progressives of the period, a partisan of the French Revolution. The Germany of that time was hardly brilliant, and here was Napoleon, who was going to forge the United States of Europe . . . In 1807, in *The Phenomenology of the Spirit*, Hegel considered Napoleon as "the soul of the world."

The book retraces the cultural odyssey of the individual, of the universal man. How shall I move from pure and simple sensation to an understanding of the culture in which I live, of the history in which I find myself? The transition is made in a series of dialectical degrees. One passes through sensation, judgment, self-awareness, stoicism, skepticism . . .

---

[1] *Notes on the Dialectics of Hegel*, trans. by H. Lefebvre, Gallimard, p. 175.

One even contemplates the Greek world, the Roman world, the 17th century, the 18th century, the Reign of Terror, Kant . . . the various religions, and finally arrives at the concept of absolute knowledge, the discovery of the very roots of science. "The concept abolishes time," Hegel then stated. When this odyssey has been understood, one can accede to absolute knowledge, and this absolute knowledge is capable of understanding history.

The last section preceding absolute knowledge is the Christian religion. Hegel was originally a theologian, not an "atheist" as Kojev has said. His purpose was to reply to Kant, who separated the "*noumen*" from the phenomenon. Man is capable of understanding history. This reflection on history relies on Christianity and the Christian dogmas. Hegel's dialectics have as their source the Trinity, the Incarnation, the Redemption. One comprehends history when one is capable of comprehending Christ, of moving from the Christian dogmas to the philosophical concepts they contain under the form of an image.

No one understood Hegel's *Phenomenology* in his own time. But later on, Marx, studying in 1834-35, was able to get quite a lot out of it.

After *Phenomenology* (1807), Hegel had announced as the second part of the system of learning, a logic, a philosophy of nature, a philosophy of the mind. His point of view was at the outset horizontal, temporal; it followed the stages of the individual more or less in reference to historical stages. Then, it was a question of setting forth the absolute logic of history. This logic would reveal God's mind before the creation of any spirit, of any nature, therefore, would understand God before eternity. God begets his Son, and this Son is, identically, nature. Nature is God's "alter ego," the fall of the mind, of the idea. This idea, become time, space, movement, has life within it, is capable of reconstituting itself, of developing into an astrological, a physical, a vegetal system . . . and finally, man intervenes. Therefore, nature produces man, and man has a history. The meaning of this history is the reconquest of its unity with nature through participation in the absolute mind. Hegel is therefore a mystic; his is a mystique of the intellect in which it is a question of achieving unity with God though philosophical meditation.

Briefly then: 1) *logic*—2) *nature*—3) *history*, with the last effecting unity between 1 and 2.

From this horizontal point of view, Hegel moved in 1812 to a vertical point of view. *History* becomes *Mind*. Now history holds only a very small place; it is not a matter of understanding it, nor is there any need to do so, since the philosopher participates immediately in the comprehension of God, in the vertical of time.

There was another modification which will explain how Marxism was able to make use of Hegelianism: "Everything that is real," Hegel said in 1817, "everything that exists, is rational." The philosopher has no need to create a world, but to understand what it is; it is when a world is in its decline that the philosopher is able to understand it. "Minerva's bird only rises at twilight," that is to say, the philosopher only understands the world in which he lives at the moment when this world is about to be replaced by another.

Marx understood *The Phenomenology of the Spirit*. In *German Ideology*, he wrote: "In spite of its original speculative defect, *Phenomenology of the Spirit* characterizes the human conditions of society." Above all, Marx took from Hegel a notion which is at the root of Marxism: the *dialectic of the master and the slave.*

From this, he fashioned two ideas:

—man creates himself by his work.

—history is the history of the class struggle.

Let us examine how, by setting forth this dialectic which consists of two phases: struggle to the death, and work.

First Phase—How is self-awareness born? To explain this dialectic, I shall take as an example two pre-human animals. How is the self to be born in these two animals? In view of the fact that the pre-human animal is defined as the power to seize, to "comprehend," and that "to seize and comprehend," for a child or an animal, is to destroy the object, to eat it, then if two of these animals meet, there necessarily results a *struggle to the death*, since each, as far as the other is concerned, is only an object to be seized, to be repudiated. What will come of this? If one of them kills the other, there will be nothing new. So that there can be something, an anthropogenesis, a genesis of humanity, one of the two must be struck with fear, with anguish, at the prospect of death, and in this anguish, he must wish to save himself and so will beg the other to spare him. Thus, something extremely important occurs: the conqueror, who has not feared death, perceives in the terror of the other his own absolute power over others and over himself, he sees himself as transcending nature, as a free being. He has been able to say: "Anything, even death, rather than slavery," whereas the other has said, "anything, even slavery, rather than death."

This is what differentiates men. The result of this is that the conquered acknowledges the conqueror as the absolute master of his life, and is condemned to the latter's service.

We live this dialectic every day as individuals, but also on a national scale during war. An armistice is an unequal and non-reciprocal acknowledgement. (An analysis found also in Sartre, applied to a conscience which looks through a keyhole and is afraid to be seen. Simone de Beauvoir puts it thus: "Every conscience seeks the negation of the other.")

The roots of history are here.

Second Phase—Now it is the reverse: the time of work. The conqueror has his conquered victim in chains. He cannot keep him this way—he would die after a few days. Since he wants to preserve this being, which makes him aware of his power, of his freedom, he must let it live, and therefore, must loosen its bonds so that it may just move and work for its master. The vanquished has become a slave because he loved life and did not want to risk his skin. The loser must live, but he lives only under the torment of death. And so he reflects and begins to think that life is not worth living without freedom; he thereby comes closer to the master. In addition, he is subject to a strict discipline, which goes against all the instincts by which he had theretofore been guided. Then Hegel quotes this saying: "The fear of the Lord is the beginning of wisdom," indicating thereby the biblical, therefore Christian, origin of his dialectic of the master and the slave.

Finally, if the slave does discipline his instincts, it is because he works. He is obliged to struggle against inhuman nature in order to give it shape, to transform it into a humanized nature. But the products of his work are for the master. This is why the dispossessed slave has to reflect on his situation, on what he has done, and realize that he is capable of doing it over again. He is beginning to become intelligent.

The master, for his part, is idle and devoted to pleasure. In the end, he must become the slave of the slave, and the slave, the master of the master.

Marx used this very profound analysis of Hegel's, but he reversed the two moments of the dialectic. The first historical fact is work. The struggle to the death is postponed until the end of history, when the capitalists have been reduced to a very small number.

In this Marxist perspective, therefore, the Hegelian dialectic is distorted. It was straightened out again by a proletarian trained by the Marxist unions of Vienna, Adolf Hitler, who wrote in *Mein Kampf*: "The first fundamental historical act is the struggle to the death, the war waged by the Master Race." Thus, he took a course opposite that of Marxism.

II. *How did Marxism become an atheistic religion?*

At Hegel's death, the unity of his system disappeared. On the one side, there was the Hegelian Right, faithful disciples who repeated the master's formulas; on the other, the Left, the wrong-headed ones. Among them was Feuerbach, author of *The Essence of Christianity*. No one has seen God. What we know is a visible humanity. God is an imaginary projection by man of his own impotence. Everything that man does not have he projects into God.

Marx accepted this demystification of Hegel's absolute Mind. Then he came to Paris where he met Engels in 1844, and like him, began to concern himself with economic questions. He lived on the rue Vaneau in Paris, where he met Proudhon, Pierre Leroux . . . In his manuscripts, published subsequently, one notes the role of *Phenomenology*. Man creates himself in his history. Why? Because he is capable of conquering nature by his work. However, there are men who work extremely hard, and the more they work, the more they are deprived of everything. This is the analysis of the *alienations*, the chief one of which is the alienation of private property. There is a separation in the appropriation of property between the one who can consume the object and the one who produces it. In *Das Kapital*, Marx explained this system of "scientific socialism." But his basic idea is not economic; it is philosophical and even primarily religious. "Philosophy," he wrote, "must be implemented. Philosophy must become a world." He reproached Hegel's philosophy for having remained such, instead of informing reality. Philosophy must transform the world. For this, materialism and history have to be tightly welded together, something Feuerbach did not do.

How was the Hegelian philosophy to be implemented in history? A mover of history had to be found for this. Marx stated it in 1844: "It is the proletariat which is capable of changing history . . . Philosophy is the head of the Revolution, the proletariat is its heart."

Marxism is based on the idea of work which transforms nature and of the struggle needed to make this transformation serve to eliminate private property. Accordingly, Marx gave his definition: "Communism becomes the real appropriation of the human essence by man and for man . . . it is a perfect naturalism and humanism. It is the veritable end of the quarrel between man and nature, and between man and man . . . It resolves the mystery of history, and knows that it is resolving it."[1]

Here, the religious character of Marxism is introduced. It is necessary to change history on the Christian bases of Hegel's philosophy.

At the moment Marx is attributing to the proletariat the power of being this moving force for transformation, the proletariat does not exist: "It is necessary," he said, "to *form* a class with radical chains . . . a sphere universal in character through its universal sufferings . . . a class that is the dissolution of all classes." Here is the very idea of the Redemption. This is why Marxism is religiously atheistic.

Jaurès was already expounding this basically Marxist idea in 1903: "The proletariat is the rock on which the church of the future will be built, it is the modern savior. The proletariariat bears as an ever-burdensome law, the law of oppression of capitalism . . . it is the cliff against which the forces of reaction are breaking from now on."[1]

III. *How does atheistic Marxism act on Christians?*

It is sufficient to take the recent example of the worker-priests, and to reflect on what one hundred priests sent among the masses, and recalled after ten or fifteen years, represent for the Church. How many rebels then? The Communists rejoice: it is the social being, the environment, they say, which creates the conscience, not ideology.

In the letter signed in 1954 by the 38 worker-priests of the Paris Mission, one may read: ". . . *the working class is*

---

[1] *Selected Writings*, Gallimard, p. 129.

[1] For these various texts and references, cf. *On Historical Actuality*, vol. II, pp. 168-173.

one . . ." We are confronted here with a fidelity to the working class balanced off in the conscience of a believer against fidelity to the Church. It is an impossible choice. In fact, it is only for Marx and the Marxists that "the working class" is *one*—and these priests failed to see it. A unity formed by their contact with universal nature, through their work. While the working class is one in this sense, it is also *universal* and capable of bringing together all men—workers, peasants, intellectuals; the middle classes (i.e. the "bourgeoisie") will have disappeared. This class is therefore *charged with the historical destiny of the universe*. It is because the worker-priests had this awareness that they were able to put it into the balance against the Church. "The working class is one" is, in fact, an affirmation of Marxist atheism, which ends up determining the Christian conscience of the priest by the proletarian conscience. At that point, "the working class" has the same features, the same "notes" as the Church, and it is capable, for the "proletarian conscience," of achieving heaven on earth.[1]

In the light of this concrete example, Madeleine Delbrel said: "The priests confused two things: the proletariat *and* Marxism. This is a semantic trap"[2] which causes people not to know what they are talking about.

It is through these words that atheism infiltrates. Madeleine Delbrel again: "The worker-priests made three discoveries: that of *poverty*, that of *justice*, and that of the sense of *history*." Three ambiguous words. Christian *poverty* and Marxist poverty face in opposite directions: Christian

---

[1] Something which Madeleine Delbrel saw very clearly. Cf. *op. cit.*, pp. 50-52. For Proudhon, the working class was always national. He used to say the working *classes*.

[2] *Op. cit.*, pp. 70-71.

poverty is a detachment from things through attachment to God; Marxist poverty is a desire for things. Under the term *justice*, one may understand the justice which is a *human* virtue, giving to each his due; for the Marxists, there is, over and above that, *class* justice, the goal of the Communist party. To this, *Chirstian* justice is radically opposed for it is not content merely to fight against injustice, it knows that it will never conquer it completely, and it is even capable of suffering injustice in a spirit of Redemption.

Sense of *history*: the Marxist is persuaded that he understands history; he believes that the union of Man and Nature will come about through work and the class struggle. But the Man-Nature unity is a false transcendence, born of the Man-God unity. For the Christian, the Man-God unity is that which is accomplished in his faith and within the Church. Marxism has perverted this Man-God unity by replacing God with Nature. Also, the Proletariat, along with the Communist Party, its guide, has assumed the form of *a* Church.

This is why and how Communism is religiously atheistic.

9. JEAN DANIELOU, S.J.

THE TRANSCENDENCE OF CHRISTIANITY

In making a study of the great non-Christian religions—Hinduism, Islamism, Buddhism—one finds at the same time a problem which cannot be avoided, that of the confrontation between these religions and Christianity. It is this decisive question that we should like to take up here. We do not intend to set forth Christianity as it is in itself, but to see how we can best represent to ourselves its relation to the other religions.

The existence of Hindu speculation on three divinities or on the symbolism of the cross, for example, raises for us the question of the possible relation of these doctrines to the Christian Trinity or to the cross of Jesus Christ. The good we derive from reading a certain Hindu or Moslem mystic makes us think carefully about the specific character of the Christian mystics and, at times, we might be tempted to say with Simone Weil: "In fact, the mystics of almost all religious traditions resemble one another, nearly to the point of identity" (*Letter to a Religious*, p. 49).

The two temptations which lie in wait here for the Christian, that of disdain and that of syncretism, are both dangerous and difficult to overcome. It is accordingly necessary to delineate the problem carefully and, while doing justice to the values of the pagan religions, to see how Christianity goes beyond them.

The first trait which characterizes Christianity is that it is faith in an event, that of the Incarnation and Resurrection of Christ. This event constitutes an intervention of God in history which radically changes the human condition and is an absolute novelty. Now this distinguishes Christianity completely from all the other religions. To reduce it, as René Guénon does, to merely one of the forms of the primitive tradition, is precisely to empty it of its original element. The great non-Christian religions affirm the existence of an eternal world opposed to the world of time. They know nothing about an intervention of the eternal in time which gives time consistency and transforms it into history.

This intervention constitutes a thenceforth irrevocable promotion, an irreversible acquisition, so that man shall nevermore be able to turn back. Nothing will be able to separate the union in Jesus Christ of the divine nature and human nature. From that time forward, there is a past and a future in the complete sense of those words. The world becomes organized into a history of which the divine interventions form the decisive acts. From the Creation to the Resurrection of Jesus Christ, passing through the election of Abraham, the Christian Revelation is that of a sacred history, the history of the "*mirabilia Dei*," the "marvelous deeds of God." The Bible is the documentation of this history. And it is remarkable that, alone of all the sacred Books, that of the Christians is a history and not an exposition of doctrines.

This history does not consist merely of ancient events. The New Testament is continued among us in the sacraments of the Church. The Christian is someone who is aware of living at the heart of sacred history, in a world in which God never ceases to act, to intervene, to perform His admirable actions, those which are fulfilled in the conversion and sanctification of hearts. That is the real history, more real than that of empires or inventions, a history in which the incorruptible Body of Christ is fashioned mysteriously through the activity of supernatural charity.

This history appears as constituting a plan ordered to an end, which is the glorification of God and the sanctification of man. It is accomplished in Jesus Christ. In Him, Creation achieved its goal, the world became successful. In this sense, He is the "novissimus Adam," ever the newest man. It is a characteristic feature of the Christian view of the world than no new event shall ever bring us anything as important as Jesus Christ; thus, the concept of some religion of the future, with Christianity as but a stage leading to it, is excluded. One does not go beyond Jesus Christ.

Nevertheless, while the order of things instituted in Jesus Christ is the final one, it involves interior growth. The Incarnation started it. But it awaits its fulfilment. This fulfilment will be the Parousia, the last event in the history of salvation. It will be characterized by the reverberation throughout the entire cosmos of the Resurrection of Jesus Christ, which heretofore has produced its effects only in the world of souls. And so Christianity, even after the Incarnation, remains an eschatology. It is the expectation of an ultimate intervention by God taking up His work again in order to bring it to its final conclusion.

We have said that Christianity was faith in an intervention by God in the world, in Jesus Christ. Now we come to a second affirmation, namely, that only this action of God's can save man, that is, that there is no salvation outside of Jesus Christ. This is what is overlooked by a position, derived from a kind of syncretism, which believes that the mystiques of all religions "meet one another even to identity." The breadth of this view seduces certain minds, which contrast it with Christian intransigence. But, in affirming that the mystiques of all religions are similar, it is saying in effect that what saves is the ascetical effort at detachment and union with God, and not the efficacy of the Cross in Jesus Christ. Once again, we are faced with a radical opposition.

What we are saying here should not be misunderstood. In no way is it a question of deprecating the examples of interior life and of detachment which we find in non-Christian religions. China, along with the doctrines of Confucius, has brought us some admirable rules of wisdom for relations among men. India offers us the example of a people who have always seen in asceticism and contemplation the highest ideal. Nor can one read its masters, from the author of the Bhaghavad Gita to Aurobindo, without experiencing the feeling of the unreality of worldly goods and of the sovereign reality of the invisible world. It is understandable that, in our modern Western world, which is concerned only with harnessing the energies of the cosmos, and which has absorbed from Marxism the illusion that man can be transformed by changing his material living conditions, the wisdom of India attracts souls thirsting for silence and the interior life.

But the fact remains that this assumes that man is able to reach God by his own powers. Christianity must categorically deny this, for two reasons. The first is the reality of original sin. This consists in a separation between man and God, which man cannot abolish by himself. It is not enough, therefore, to say that man alienated himself by turning toward the exterior world, and that he has only to turn aside from the life of the body to discover the pure spirituality which is his very being. For Christianity, it is not the body which is the principle of sin, but the whole man, soul and body, is the captive of evil and God alone can liberate him from this captivity, through grace.

The second reason is that the Christian God is absolutely inaccessible. He alone can, therefore, introduce man to this participation in His nature which supernatural life is. For Hinduism, in fact, or neo-Platonism, the soul is divine by nature, and it only needs to move away from what is alien to it in order to find God by finding itself. But this concept assumes that there is no radical distinction between the uncreated God and the created spirit. The mystique of India presupposes a certain pantheism. On the other hand, the first article of Christian faith is the doctrine of the Creator-God, that is, the radical distinction between God and man. Accordingly, God alone is able to raise man to this participation in Him which is the supernatural life, the apex of which is the mystical life. It is inaccessible to any human asceticism.

The fundamental reversal of perspectives is clear. For syncretism, the saved are the interior souls, regardless of the religion to which they may belong. For Christianity, the saved are those who believe, regardless of their level of interior life. A little child, a worker weighed down by his labors, if they believe, are superior to the greatest ascetics. "We are not great religious personalities," as Guardini put it so well, "we are servants of the Word." Christ had already said that, while St. John the Baptist might be "the greatest among the sons of men, yet the least of the sons of the kingdom is greater than he." It is possible that there are in the world some great religious personalities outside Christianity; it may even happen that at a given time, the greatest religious personalities will be found outside Christianity. This is of no consequence. What does matter, is obedience to the words of Jesus Christ.

In this light, the difference between non-Christian mystiques and the Christian mystique appears. For the former, union with God is the goal of an asceticism through which the soul, stripping itself of what is alien to it, discovers its pure essence, which is God Himself. The emphasis will therefore be placed on ascetical techniques: exercises of recollection, unification of the soul, etc. It happens that Christian mystics make use of these methods. But they are always secondary, and they are never sufficient. The Christian God is, in fact, a living and transcendent God whom no technique could ever reach. He communicates Himself freely, when and as He wishes. The mystical experience is not conditioned upon any technique. Thus, the grace of God strikes Paul enroute to Damascus, enters the soul of Marie of the Incarnation rolling casks on the Loire docks. It has no other source than the sovereign liberty of the divine love. It is not so much psychological exercises which dispose the soul to receive it as it is the religious attitudes which render the soul pleasing to God.

Up to now, we have stressed primarily Christianity's nature as a divine fact. But its transcendence is also apparent on the level of doctrines. This fact is disregarded by a third type of syncretism which believes it can find the main Christian dogmas, the Trinity, the Redemption, etc., in other religions. Thus, there are a number of comparisons the superficiality of which has been demonstrated many times and which no serious mind should retain, but which continue to be spread, sowing some uncertainty in the minds of many of our contemporaries, which dilutes the faith. It is astonishing that Simone Weil, otherwise gifted with a very sharp critical sense, should have yielded to this temptation. In her *Letter to a Religious*, she repeats a large share of these slogans.

Thus, she compares the words of Christ: "I am the true vine," to the role of the vine in the cult of Dionysos (p. 21). But it has been established that we are dealing here with two different themes: the Palestinian theme of the vine as the figure of the people of God (Isaias 5:1), and the Greek theme in which the vine symbolizes immortality, in connection with drunkenness. The maternity of the Virgin is compared to the mother goddesses of antiquity. Yet it is certain that the cult of the Virgin in Christianity stems from the historical role of Mary in the plan of salvation, and not from a sublimation of femininity, as in the religions of nature. The death of Christ on the Cross is compared to the crucifixion of the soul of the world in Plato's *Timeus* (p. 23). It is clear, however, that the role of the Cross in Christianity derives from the gibbet on which Jesus was sacrificed, which was in the form of a T. In no way does it come from the symbolism of the four dimensions which is found in various religions. The Christian Trinity is compared to the Greek triads (p. 27) and the Hindu triads (p. 33). But it is certain that, far from proceeding from a dialectical requirement, the Trinity constitutes a stumbling block as far as reason is concerned, for it is not a question of a primordial unity and its manifestations, but of Three Persons Who subsist eternally in the unity of one nature.

I cannot take more than a word here to indicate the essential contrast for each of these points. It has often happened that Christianity has utilized in its liturgy symbols borrowed from the religions of nature. Thus, in the third century A.D., Hippolyte of Rome gave the cross a cosmic symbolism. The language of the pagan mysteries was employed for the sacraments beginning in the fourth century. The catacomb paintings show us the vine as a symbol of immortality. And in our own time, Father Monchanin proposes to designate the Trinity by means of the sacred formula *saccidânanda*, which describes the Hindu triad. But those are secondary developments and cultural adaptations. Insofar as their origins are concerned, the Christian dogmas are a new revelation.

Does this mean that the natural religions have not attained certain truths concerning God? Such a statement would be inaccurate. St. Paul himself teaches that "since the creation of the world, the invisible perfections of God are known through visible things." The non-Christian religions have been able to grasp that which human reason left to itself is capable of discovering, that is, God's exterior, His existence and His perfections as they are manifest through His action in the world.

But there is something no reason has ever been able to suspect, a threshold no foot has ever crossed, a darkness where no one enters by stealth: it is the mystery of the inner life of God. The depths of the Trinity are absolutely inaccessible to man and only the Son of God has been able to introduce man thereto: "No one has ever seen God. But the only Son, who is in the bosom of the Father, he has made him known to us." We have reached the heart of what constitutes the irreducible originality of Christianity, namely, the fact that the Son of God, having come among us, has revealed to us these two truths, which are closely joined to one another: the presence of this mysterious life of love in God called the Trinity, and our own calling, in Him and through Him, to participate eternally in this life. It is summed up in one person, the person of Jesus Christ, God made man, in Whom can be found all that we must know. The religions of nature—and this is what is valuable about them—testify to man's movement toward God; Christianity is the movement of God Who, in Jesus Christ, comes to take man in order to lead him to Himself.

Thus, compared with Christianity, the pagan religions seem out of date and distorted. Still, they contain some worthwhile elements. Would not their disappearance then be an impoverishment? Simone Weil feared that it would: "If the other traditions disappear from the surface of the earth," she wrote, "it would be an irreparable loss. As it is, the missionaries have already caused too many to disappear." (p. 35.) Against this accusation, we must set forth the true concept of the Christian mission. Pius XII enunciated it thus in the encyclical *Divini Praecones*: "The Church has never treated the doctrines of the pagans with contempt and disdain; rather, she has freed them from all error, then completed them and crowned them with Christian wisdom."

This formula admirably sums up the attitude of Christianity. It does not treat the religious values of the pagan religions with disdain. But it first purifies them from all error, that is, it destroys the corruption—especially idolatry. This is why conversion will always be a rupture. Progress from paganism to Christianity is never accomplished through homogeneous evolution. Then, Christianity, through Christian wisdom, completes and fulfills the imperfect truths which exist in the pagan religions. It takes up the natural values of the religious man, it recovers them in order to consecrate them. Thus, we find early Christianity integrating the values of Greek philosophy after having purified them. Thus shall we be able to see in the future, Christianity assuming all the values contained in the asceticism of the Hindus or the wisdom of Confucius, after having purified them. The Christian mission, when it is what it is supposed to be, is not destruction, but liberation and transformation of the religious values of paganism. Christ did not come to destroy, but to fulfill.